Wait Here and Watch

Wait Here and Watch

A Eucharistic Commentary on the Passion According to St. Matthew

Bonnie Bowman Thurston

Eugene, Oregon

Unless otherwise indicated, all scripture quotations are from the Revised Standard Version of the Bible, copyrighted 1946, 1952, © 1971, 1973 by the Division of Christian Education of the National Council of Churches of Christ in America.

Wipf and Stock Publishers
199 W 8th Ave, Suite 3
Eugene, OR 97401

Wait Here and Watch
A Commentary on the Passion According to St. Matthew
By Thurston, Bonnie B.
Copyright©1989 by Thurston, Bonnie Bowman
ISBN: 1-59244-769-4
Publication date 7/27/2004
Previously published by CBP Press, 1989

For

Burton Bradford Thurston, Sr.

Who, above all things,
loves the Lord and his Table
1 Corinthians 5:7-8

Contents

Introduction 8

The Gospel of Matthew 10
    Setting 10
    Author 11
    Date and Place of Composition 12
    Sources 13
    Structure 14
    Literary Features 15
    Theological Aims and Concerns 16

Commentary on the Text 17
    Chapter 26 17
    Chapter 27 47
    Chapter 28 82

Notes 93

Works Consulted 95

Introduction

If one were to describe this work in horticultural terms, "hybrid" is the word that would come to mind. This exposition of the Passion narrative in Matthew is intended to be both a commentary and a devotional work. It attempts to present in simple language the conclusions of modern scholarship and at the same time serve as a meditation on the events of the Lord's Passion. So scholarship and devotion "cross–pollinate" in these pages.

Many members of the clergy, pastors, and laypersons are called upon to present remarks or to focus the thoughts of a congregation before the Eucharistic celebration. This volume is written to help them do that.

Furthermore, many people seek to have their own experience of the Lord's Supper made more meaningful. For them, this book can serve as a private devotional manual. Along with their Bibles, it will heighten their understanding of what is done at the Table. Because Lent is a special time of remembrance and examination, the focus on the Passion in this little volume may make it an especially helpful devotional guide at this season.

Matthew's account of the Passion has been chosen for

exposition because, in the tradition, Matthew is "the church's book." This evangelist has had a special interest in the life and order of the Christian community, and so to this evangelist we turn to find insight into our distinctively Christian ritual act.

For readers interested in the more scholarly aspects of this study, or for readers who would benefit from placing these remarks in their original context, the following general introduction to Matthew is included.

The Gospel of Matthew

Setting

The setting of Matthew is very important for understanding the intent and message of the gospel. We are fairly confident that Mark was written about the time of the Jewish War and the destruction of the temple, or between A.D. 66 and 70. Matthew was probably written fifteen years thereafter. In the intervening time, what could have affected the Christian message?

First was the rise to primacy of Pharisaic Judaism. Sources for the period are murky, but apparently the Pharisees under Rabbi Johannan ben Zakkai fled Jerusalem and convened at Jamnia near the Mediterranean coast. Here the foundations of rabbinic Judaism were laid; that is, rabbis assumed authority as interpreters of the Law, which was codified into the canon of Jewish scripture.

Prior to the Jewish War, Christians who were Jews had remained in the synagogue and within the boundaries of Judaism. However, after A.D. 70, the rabbis began to devise what might be called "tests of faith." About A.D. 85, the time of the writing of Matthew, the twelfth benediction was added to the Tefillah:

> For persecutors let there be no hope, and the dominion of arrogance do thou speedily root out in our days; and let Christians and minim ["heretics"] perish in a moment, let them be blotted out of the living and let them not be written with the righteous.

If one hesitated to say this prayer or Amen to it, one was expelled from the synagogue. Essentially, Christians were excluded from Judaism.

In *The Setting of the Sermon on the Mount*,[1] W.D. Davies sets forth the notion that Matthew, and especially the Sermon on the Mount, was a sort of Christian response to Jamnia. Matthew was attempting to define Christian identity over against the reforms of Jamnia by taking up many of the concerns of the rabbis there, for example, the fall of Jerusalem and the infidelity of the city.

Some questions that arise, then, are: Who wrote Matthew, a Jew or a Gentile? Where was Matthew written? Was the community in which it was written in, or out of, the synagogue?

Author

According to the traditions of Papias and Irenaeus, the author of Matthew was one of the Twelve, who is identified as a tax collector in Matthew 10:3 (cf. Luke 6:15; Mark 3:18; Acts 1:13). This is highly unlikely. Why would an eyewitness of the events in question have relied so heavily on the Markan account? Scholarly consensus asserts that Mark preceded Matthew and Luke. However, the suggestion of Robert Gundry that Matthew took notes on Jesus' words and wrote his gospel early, between A.D. 50 and 60, is tempting.[2]

Most commentators assume Matthew was a Jewish Christian on the basis of his interests, Jewish roots and genealogies, affirmation of the Law and the Prophets and extensive quotation from that material, and his insistence that Jesus' mission was to "the lost sheep of the house of Israel."

It is probably most fruitful to think of Matthew as a "Christian scribe," a learned layman who took over from the rabbis the task of applying the law. If Matthew 13:52 is not the author's description of himself, it fits him well.

Date and Place of Composition

The Griesbach hypothesis suggested that Matthew was the first gospel written, but that theory is no longer widely held.[3] Thus the date of Matthew depends on that of Mark.

Mark cannot be earlier than A.D. 40, since chapter 13 of that gospel appears to reflect Caligula's attempt to profane the temple. Nor can it be much later than A.D. 70.

In A.D. 115, Ignatius mentions Matthew, so that would be the latest date for that gospel. Matthew 22 is frequently taken to refer to the destruction of the temple, and we have noted the historical framework following that sad event. Thus we can say with some assurance that Matthew was written between 80 and 115, probably between 85 and 90. Matthew depends upon Mark, has the theological concerns of a second generation Christian, and shows the influence of events at Jamnia (for example, in the constant reference to "their" synagogue).

Again, it is impossible to locate the exact place of

Matthew's composition. Its origins may well have been Palestinian; it certainly uses Palestinian and Jerusalem traditions. Many scholars suggest Antioch in Syria (or a community east of there) as a place of origin. Jack Dean Kingsbury summarizes the arguments for Antioch when he notes that it contained a mixed population of Gentiles and Jews, that it was a prosperous and urban community (Matthew refers to cities twenty-six times, Mark only four; when he refers to money, Matthew escalates the amounts in Mark), and that Matthew's Greek reflects that of a native speaker and not that of a translation.[4]

Other suggested locations include Alexandria, because of Matthew's tradition of the flight to Egypt, and Caesarea Maritima, the port city of Herod and an early center of Christian learning.

Sources

Although the theory is challenged by some, the basic assumption is that Matthew used Mark, "Q," and a source of his own, which is called "M."

The fact that Matthew follows Mark to such a large extent is a witness to his respect for that work. Matthew seldom alters the sayings of Jesus in Mark, although he rearranges and abbreviates Mark, especially Mark's accounts of the miracles. Matthew's theological interests lead him to insist on faith as a presupposition for Jesus' help, to idealize the Twelve, and to exalt Jesus as Lord and eliminate any offensive reports about him.

The Q material in Matthew is attested by the often quoted and frequently debated statement of Papias that "Matthew compiled the logia in the Hebrew language and each one interpreted them as he was able." This has led to endless speculation, in particular to the suggestion that Matthew was originally written in Hebrew.

The M material is usually divided into discourse material and special narrative material (birth stories, Petrine material, and Passion and resurrection stories).[5]

Structure

There are a number of theories about the structure of Matthew. In many ways the most satisfying is the classic formulation by Benjamin Bacon, the "Pentateuchal theory," which suggests that Matthew is organized into five blocks of teaching material.[6]

At Matthew 7:28; 11:1; 13:53; 19:1; and 26:1 we find the phrase:"And it happened when Jesus finished these sayings . . . " (or one similar). These phrases mark off five "lectures" of Jesus. In the early chapters of Matthew, the evangelist draws a number of parallels between Jesus and Moses, and this structure continues that comparison by creating a Christian pentateuch.

The following structure of Matthew, then, seems plausible:

Book I (chapters 3—7)
    narrative (3—4): ministry of Jesus
    sermon (5—7): Sermon on the Mount

Book II (chapters 8—10)
    narrative (8—9): authority of Jesus
    sermon (10): missionary discourse

Book III (chapters 11—13)
    narrative (11—12): coming of Kingdom
    discourse (13): teaching in parables

Book IV (chapters 14—18)
    narrative (14—17): life in community
    discourse (18): Christian community regulations

Book V (chapters 19—25)
    narrative (19—23): consummation of the age
    discourse (24—25): apocalyptic discourse

Passion (26—28)

This fivefold organization presents us with a new Torah for Christians that exhibits special concern for Christian community. Matthew wants to prove that Jesus is the fulfillment of Jewish expectations and the consummation of their history. Among the gospel writers, it is Matthew who most frequently refers to the Old Testament. Matthew refers to Jesus as Son of David and emphasizes that his messiahship is not as expected.

Literary Features

Within this theological structure, Matthew as a writer relies heavily on formula statements, quotation, the use of "then" rather than Mark's "and," and "kingdom of heaven" rather than "kingdom of God." Matthew characteristically refers to "their" synagogue (indicating exclusion of Christians). He is fond of derogatory terms like "hypocrite" and "of little faith" as well as commendatory references to "little ones," "brethren," and "children" in the Christian community.

Theological Aims and Concerns

While it is true that Matthew intends to defend Christian faith against its Jewish opponents and to instruct converts from paganism in the ethical implications of their new religion, neither statement of Matthew's aims is complete. Gerhard Barth completes our understanding by reminding us that the evangelist was engaged in a struggle on two fronts. To Christians who dismissed the Law altogether, Matthew stressed its enduring validity. And to those steeped in Pharasaic background who were too rigid, Matthew stressed the "law of love."[7] Matthew seeks to help those inside the church to live a life of love and fellowship that follows the example of their Lord's life.

Matthew is the only evangelist to use the technical term for church (*ecclesia*), and he includes a discourse on Christian community life (chapter 18). For this reason Matthew's Passion narrative was chosen for this treatment. The characteristic phrase that he uses to describe the bond between the Christian community and the risen Christ is "with us" or "with you." Surely, Christ is most with us in the Eucharist, so we shall focus on this experience as we examine Matthew 26—28.

Commentary on the Text

Matthew 26:1–2

¹When Jesus had finished all these sayings, he said to his disciples, ²"You know that after two days the Passover is coming, and the Son of man will be delivered up to be crucified."

Matthew's account of the Passion of Jesus begins immediately after he completes the fifth of the five discourses that characterize the first gospel.[8] This last discourse has been strongly apocalyptic in tone. Its themes have been suffering and mercy.

These two are also the great themes of the last Passion prediction, which Jesus utters in these verses, and they are the great themes of the passion story itself.[9]

Jesus makes a very clear statement about what is to come, but his words contain a great paradox. Passover is the time of deliverance and freedom from bondage. It is a time when the Jews recall the most dramatic example of God's merciful intervention in history on their behalf. But Jesus says this Passover is to be a deliverance unto death.

The Hebrew word for Passover, *pesach*, means "to leap over," "to save," "to show mercy." The Greek word for Passover, *paschein*, means "to suffer."

The events that unfold in Matthew 26—28 tell of suffering and of mercy. This is the story we remember as we gather on the first day of the week. Set before us are the symbols of the Passover, blood and unleavened bread. They symbolize God's leap over all that has separated us from God. These symbols of mercy are also symbols of suffering, the outpoured blood and broken body of the Savior.

Here are the symbols of our deliverance from slavery and bondage. May we receive them with grateful hearts.

Matthew 26:3-5

³Then the chief priests and the elders of the people gathered in the palace of the high priest, who was called Caiaphas, ⁴and took counsel together in order to arrest Jesus by stealth and kill him. ⁵But they said, "Not during the feast, lest there be a tumult among the people."

In the first five verses of chapter 26, Matthew introduces the major characters and the setting of the Passion narrative. The setting is that of the Passover and the major players are Jesus, his disciples, the Sanhedrin, Caiaphas, and the crowds gathered in Jerusalem to celebrate the feast.

Verses 3-5 begin the fulfillment of the prediction Jesus has uttered. The highest court in the land, the Sanhedrin, has gathered for an informal meeting in the courtyard of the high priest's house. The image is one that is all too familiar to us, that of plot and intrigue in high places.

The choices open to these plotters are limited. They

could not entrap Jesus by argument or discredit him with the government. They fear attempting to take him by force because of the people. Either the people are Jesus' followers and would defend him or, because of political animosity at this time, there was danger of a riot that would lead to Roman intervention and the Sanhedrin's loss of power (cf. John 11:47–48). And so the decision is made to arrest Jesus by stealth, to seize him apart from the festival with its assembly of people.

Jesus' situation as described here is also articulated by the psalmist:

Yea, I hear the whispering of many—
    terror on every side!—
as they scheme together against me,
    as they plot to take my life (Psalm 31:13).

The psalmist's next verse reveals Jesus' response:

But I trust in thee, O Lord,
    I say, "Thou art my God."
My times are in thy hand . . . (Ps. 31:14–15a).

Many innocent people have been undone by conspiracy in high places. Jesus and the martyrs of the church have faced what many face today: injustice, oppression, the jealousy of petty officials, conspiracy. Only one act in all human history could overcome such littleness. In only one place will we find consolation and solace in the face of overwhelming injustice. Only one table is large enough to accommodate a meal for both the oppressors and the oppressed. And we gather there in this moment.

Matthew 26:6–13

⁶Now when Jesus was at Bethany in the house of Simon the leper, ⁷a woman came up to him with an alabaster flask of very expensive ointment, and she poured it on his head, as he sat at table. ⁸But when the disciples saw it, they were indignant, saying, "Why this waste? ⁹For this ointment might have been sold for a large sum, and given to the poor." ¹⁰But Jesus, aware of this, said to them, "Why do you trouble the woman? For she has done a beautiful thing to me. ¹¹For you always have the poor with you, but you will not always have me. ¹²In pouring this ointment on my body she has done it to prepare me for burial. ¹³Truly, I say to you, wherever this gospel is preached in the whole world, what she has done will be told in memory of her."

The village of Bethany, about two miles east of Jerusalem, was apparently Jesus' headquarters during his last week. Passover crowds in the city may have made it impossible to find accommodation in Jerusalem. Or perhaps Jesus' friend, Lazarus, and his sisters had made arrangements for him at Simon's house.

It is important that Matthew tells us Simon is a leper, an outcast, unclean. Good Jews might well have thought that Jesus was in a place he ought not to have been, an unclean place. Is it because of these unusual circumstances that a woman is able to break convention and approach a rabbi?

Her gift is extravagant, an alabaster flask worth, as John's parallel tells us, 300 denarii in a time when a single denarius was a day's wage for a laborer (cf. John 12:1–8).

The disciples murmur against this "waste," and it is a mark of Jesus' divinity that he hears what was spoken inwardly.

Jesus gives this anonymous woman the highest commendation recorded in the New Testament. She has responded to him as a king who is destined to die.[10] She has lavished an extravagant gift upon the human Jesus at a time when he has been battered by controversy and distrust and must know what he faces.

And Jesus gives this woman a princely reward. Wherever the gospel is preached in the whole world, not only Jesus, but also the generosity of this woman will be remembered. (The word "When," *hopou*, suggests that Jesus knew this triumphal news would be proclaimed.) How can we fail to be moved as we read these words and, by reading, participate in our Lord's word coming true!

Jesus sits with lepers, allows women to approach, chides the short-sighted, and speaks words that come to pass. Gathered at the table, we see his extravagant gifts "poured out" for us. And here, too, we hear his words come to pass. "This is my body.... This is my blood of the covenant, which is poured out for many for the forgiveness of sins" (Matt. 26:26–28).

Matthew 26:14–16

¹⁴Then one of the twelve, who was called Judas Iscariot, went to the chief priests ¹⁵and said, "What will you give me if I deliver him to you?" And they paid him thirty pieces of silver. ¹⁶And from that moment he sought an opportunity to betray him.

Great works of literature frequently use contrast to emphasize a point. Here in Matthew we find one of the starkest contrasts in Christian history. In contrast to the beautiful gift of the unnamed woman, we turn to the betrayal and treachery of Judas, the disciple. Opposed to the perfume of great price is the cheap betrayal.

Judas, one of the Twelve, one from Jesus' "inner circle," seeks out the chief priests and actively looks for a chance to betray Jesus. As we know from verses 3–5, this is exactly what the priests hoped for.

Matthew alone mentions the thirty pieces of silver as the price offered for the betrayal. Exodus 21:32 tells us that thirty shekels of silver was the price of a slave. Zechariah, who appears as a shepherd in the text in question, says his wages are thirty shekels of silver (Zech. 11:12). The unnamed woman lavishes a gift worth ten months' wages, and a known friend betrays Jesus for the price of a slave!

As we approach the experience of Holy Communion, we do well to "count costs." Jesus suggested to the multitudes that prudent persons do so. (See Luke 14:25–30.) What has our presence here cost a loving God?

And yet we know the essence of our experience of communion is not one of prudence but of extravagance, of giving all, of outpouring. In contrast to the niggardliness of Judas, we experience the generosity of God. In contrast to thirty pieces of silver paid in betrayal, we remember a life freely given in ransom for others

Truly no man can ransom himself,
> or give to God the price of his life (Ps. 49:7).

While the Psalm is true, we know that the price is paid. In the words of the hymn by Elvina M. Hall,

Jesus died for me.
All to him I owe;
Sin had left a crimson stain,
He washed it white as snow.

Matthew 26:17–19

17Now on the first day of Unleavened Bread the disciples came to Jesus, saying, "Where will you have us prepare for you to eat the passover?" 18He said, "Go into the city to a certain one, and say to him, 'The Teacher says, My time is at hand; I will keep the passover at your house with my disciples.'" 19 And the disciples did as Jesus had directed them, and they prepared the passover.

Modern scholars face a difficult problem in seeking to harmonize what we know about Passover customs with the accounts in the four gospels.[11] But this is not Matthew's concern as he introduces the "Last Supper," which he wants understood as Passover for theological reasons. Matthew's interest here continues a theme that predominated in the gospel, that of discipleship.

Luke has told us that it was Peter and John who came to Jesus to inquire about preparations (Luke 22:8). Mark's gospel describes the cloak-and-dagger, clandestine arrangements for this meal, which were made to insure that Jesus had uninterrupted time with his disciples (Mark 14:12–16). Matthew simply indicates Jesus' foreknowledge of events as he sends the disciples off to the one with whom an agreement had previously been made. (It was the usual custom for householders in Jerusalem to rent rooms for use of pilgrims at Passover.)

Matthew omits the other details because his interest is in the disciples who "did as Jesus had directed them" (v. 19). For Matthew, obedience is the key to discipleship, the proof of faithfulness.[12] Disciples of Jesus are those who do what he commands. It is not enough to be only a hearer of the word.

When we gather at his Table, we do so in obedience to Jesus' command as it was recorded for us by Luke and Paul: "Do this in remembrance of me" (Luke 22:19; 1 Cor. 11:24). We do not simply hear of Eucharist; we are obedient to his command to participate in it.

May we always be quick, as the disciples were quick, to obey Jesus' request to prepare a Table for fellowship with him and with others.

Here at Thy table, Lord, we meet
To feed on food divine:
Thy body is the bread we eat,
Thy precious blood the wine.

He that prepares this rich repast,
Himself comes down and dies;
And then invites us thus to feast
Upon the sacrifice.

Sure, there was never love so free,
Dear Savior, so divine!
Well Thou may'st claim that heart of me,
Which owes so much to Thine.

Yes, Thou shalt surely have my heart,
My soul, my strength, my all;

With life itself I'll freely part,
My Jesus, at Thy call.

(Samuel Stennett, 1728–1795)

Matthew 26:20–25

²⁰When it was evening, he sat at table with the twelve disciples; ²¹and as they were eating, he said, "Truly, I say to you, one of you will betray me." ²²And they were very sorrowful, and began to say to him one after another, "Is it I, Lord?" ²³He answered. "He who has dipped his hand in the dish with me, will betray me. ²⁴The Son of man goes as it is written of him, but woe to that man by whom the Son of man is betrayed! It would have been better for that man if he had not been born." ²⁵Judas, who betrayed him, said, "Is it I, Master?" He said to him, "You have said so."

Conflicting emotions assault us as we look at this little scene. It opens with the warmth of a family gathering, Jesus and his disciples reclining together at a meal. But it quickly becomes a scene of sorrow and questioning, and it closes with the sure knowledge of betrayal.

Few motivations in history have raised more questions than those of Judas Iscariot.[13] What impelled him to betray Jesus? Matthew 26:15 suggests greed as a motive. John 12:4–8 implies it was loss of face. Scholars have suggested both jealousy over Jesus' popularity and impatience at Jesus' slowness to act. Was Judas operating with a positive, if flawed, motive? Did he suppose he could force Jesus' hand and bring his kingdom to pass by backing him into the corner that arrest seemed to represent?

A. Carr believes the motive that impelled Judas may have been "worldly ambition." "Jesus said of him that he was a 'devil' . . . the term that was on a special occasion applied to St. Peter, and for the same reason. Peter for a moment allowed the thought of a worldly kingdom to prevail; with Judas it was the predominant idea which. . . forced out whatever element of good he once possessed."[14]

Whatever his motive, Judas was one of Jesus' close friends, one who ate from the common bowl, dipping with Jesus and the others into the dish that may have contained the *charoseth*, the sauce of vinegar into which Passover bread and bitter herbs were dipped. Verse 25 clearly indicates that, at least in Matthew's mind, Jesus knew his betrayer. The formula of assent Jesus uses is found in Aramaic, Hebrew, and Greek.

As we prepare to partake of the elements, we are sobered by the thought that one who shared a holy meal with Jesus was also the one who betrayed him. What might lead us to betrayal? Desire for acceptability? Power? Position? As we approach his Table, we must examine our hearts to see if anything of Judas lurks there.

"Let a man examine himself, and so eat of the bread and drink of the cup" (1 Cor. 11:28).

Matthew 26:26-29

²⁶Now as they were eating, Jesus took bread, and blessed, and broke it, and gave it to the disciples and said, "Take, eat; this is my body." ²⁷And he took a cup, and when he had given thanks he gave it to them, saying, "Drink of it, all of you; ²⁸for this is my blood of the

covenant, which is poured out for many for the forgiveness of sins. 29I tell you I shall not drink again of this fruit of the vine until that day when I drink it new with you in my Father's kingdom."

We hear these words so often that the force of their meaning is sometimes lost on us. One of these familiar verses would have special meaning for those first Jewish disciples: "This is my blood of the [new] covenant, which is poured out for many for the forgiveness of sins" (v. 28).

Behind these words of our Lord stands the old covenant made at Sinai and the remembrance that God has rescued God's people in the past. Now, by the blood of Jesus, a new covenant or a new relationship is in effect.

Blood was the very stuff of life. Its "pouring out" denoted a violent death, which alone carried the value of a sacrifice. The result of this sacrifice is the remission or forgiveness of sins. As the writer of Hebrews put it, "without the shedding of blood there is no forgiveness of sins" (Heb. 9:22).

Matthew's account here reflects the sacrificial terminology of the Septuagint and bases forgiveness on the shedding of Jesus' blood. With one stroke, both the old covenant based on law and the old atonement based on the sacrifice of animals in the temple are wiped out. Fulfilled is the prophecy of Jeremiah, "Behold, the days are coming, says the Lord, when I will make a new covenant with the house of Israel. . ." (31:31).

But this new covenant is not limited to Israel. Jesus' blood is shed "for many." His command is that we all eat and drink. In his mercy, God forgives us Gentiles through the sacrifice of God's Son. The benefit of the sacrifice comes to all of us who obey Jesus' commands. This day he commands, "Take, eat, drink ye all." And we respond, "Thanks be to God!"

As we gather at the Lord's Table, we are wise to reflect upon the scene of his Passion. We must never forget what it cost him that we might share this meal. And yet our Lord himself, in the midst of his darkest hours, was able to see beyond them to what was coming. He speaks of the day "I drink it new with you in my Father's kingdom" (v. 29).

Jesus preached and taught about the kingdom of heaven; now he speaks about "the kingdom of my Father," emphasizing God's Fatherhood and his own divine sonship. Implicit in the statement is a promise, a promise that Jesus' friends will eventually be with him in his kingdom. Jesus tells the disciples, and us, that his Father's reign will come and that they will share in it. In his Father's house are many mansions; what he does prepares them for his followers. Jesus' presence with his disciples in the upper room insures their presence with him in the kingdom.

In the midst of the sadness of separation, which causes Jesus to abstain from drinking wine with his friends, comes the promise of a reunion at a future time. That same promise is ours. We are sobered by what the bread and wine represent, but we must not fail to be encouraged by what they promise.

God's rule will be established; God's kingdom will come; Jesus will share with us there. And it will be a "new" experience. In the twinkling of an eye, we shall be changed, and we shall share in the unseen things that these physical emblems represent.

Let us eat and drink to celebrate the fact that, however dim the process may be, however slow and mysterious, God in Christ is making all things new and bringing us who love God closer to the kingdom.

Matthew 26:30-32

³⁰And when they had sung a hymn, they went out to the Mount of Olives. ³¹Then Jesus said to them, "You will all fall away because of me this night; for it is written, 'I will strike the shepherd, and the sheep of the flock will be scattered.' ³²But after I am raised up, I will go before you to Galilee."

Jesus and his friends have finished supper. Luke tells us the meal is the Passover, which customarily closes with the singing of hymns, the Hallel from Psalms 115 to 118. Then, having walked out through the Kidron Valley, Jesus gathers his disciples for two shattering predictions.

Each of them, he says, will "stumble" because of the persecution that is coming upon him. With what he must bear, they are not even able to be associated. Jesus enforces his point with a quotation from Zechariah, the prophet who shares with Haggai the dream of a rebuilt temple, a purified community, and a messianic age. In Zechariah 13:7, God strikes the shepherd. There, a remnant is saved; they are refined by fire and become God's people.

In telling the disciples of the coming calamity, Jesus makes it clear that God's action is at the root of what happens. God scatters the sheep that they may be refined and purified. And so Jesus tells the disciples that he will be raised up. God will effect his rescue. God's action lies at the basis of Jesus' Passion. Jesus will go before the disciples into Galilee, back to the home country, the place of their ordinary daily activity.

Matthew, writing in retrospect, knew that all of the followers would stumble. Gathered at his Table, we, too, know from bitter personal experience how easy it is to deny Jesus. We, too, have faced situations where to be named Christian was a dangerous thing, an experience of loss of status. We, too, have put our pride before our Lord's Passion.

But to stumble is not to fall. The soul searching that we face when we are separated from our Lord by our own actions is God's way of refining us spiritually. As Zechariah assures us, we will call on God's name, and God will answer (Zech. 13:9).

As Jesus promised the first disciples, God raised him up. And being risen, he goes before us on our daily walk, in our ordinary circumstances, and he raises us up.

The Lord's Table is the symbol of God's action in our behalf. It challenges us to take up our sufferings in the spirit of the Christ, and it strengthens us to do so. And, when we stumble, it stands as a reminder that Christ Jesus precedes and beckons us. And we remember the words of the psalmist, "Thou preparest a table before me" (Ps. 23: 5).

Matthew 26:33-35

[33] Peter declared to him, "Though they all fall away because of you, I will never fall away." [34] Jesus said to him, "Truly, I say to you, this very night, before the cock crows, you will deny me three times." [35] Peter said to him, "Even if I must die with you, I will not deny you." And so said all the disciples.

Jesus has predicted not only the falling away of the disciples, but his being raised by God and his return to the flock. Poor, impulsive Peter! In his haste to assure Jesus of loyalty, he misses the crucial promise that Jesus makes.

For Matthew, Peter is representative of Jesus' followers. He is the first to declare Jesus the Christ. He leaps into the sea to walk to Jesus—and sinks! He is the first to swear loyalty, and the first publicly to deny Jesus.

Peter's precociousness led him to a false confidence in his own resources and abilities. Peter accomplished much for the church, but only after he had made a devastating error in judgment and lived through its consequences. Matthew tells us that when he realized what his denial of Jesus meant, Peter "wept bitterly" (26:75).

Bitterness often awaits those who trust in themselves and their own resources. None of us can be confident in and of ourselves. In 1 Corinthians, Paul reminds us there is no place for human pride in the presence of God: "no human being might boast in the presence of God" (1 Cor. 1:29).

This table reminds us of the fact that God triumphs, not by strength, but by what the world counts as weakness. "God chose what is low and despised in the world" (1 Cor. 1:28). God chose a cross. God chose Peter, a coward and a traitor to Jesus. God chooses us to bring God's kingdom to bear on this world.

Peter came to know that he could not do for himself what the body and blood of Jesus did for him. This Table enjoins us, in the words of Paul, to acknowledge our dependence: "Let him who boasts, boast of the Lord" (1 Cor. 1:31).

> We meet, as in that upper room they met;
> Thou at the table, blessing, yet dost stand;
> "This is my body:" so thou givest yet:
> Faith still receives the cup as from thy hand.

One body we, one body who partake,
One Church united in communion blest;
One name we bear, one bread of life we break,
With all thy saints on earth and saints at rest.

One with each other, Lord, for one in thee,
Who art one Saviour and one living Head;
Then open thou our eyes, that we may see;
Be known to us in breaking of the bread.

(George W. Briggs, 1875-1959)

Matthew 26:36–38

[36]Then Jesus went with them to a place called Gethsemane, and he said to his disciples, "Sit here, while I go yonder and pray." [37]And taking with him Peter and the two sons of Zebedee, he began to be sorrowful and troubled. [38]Then he said to them, "My soul is very sorrowful, even to death; remain here, and watch with me."

Jesus leads the disciples to Gethsemane, the place of the oil press, the place of his own testing. Telling the majority to rest, he takes his closest friends, Peter, James, and John, and goes a little way to pray.

Here we see a poignant, human side of our Lord, the need to have close friends nearby in a time of crisis. Here we see the Comforter seeking comfort. This is the only personal request, the only thing Jesus asks for himself in all the gospels.

Matthew describes Jesus as sorrowful and troubled.

"Troubled," *ademonein*, implies restlessness, distraction in the face of a difficulty that cannot be escaped. Then, in verse 38, Jesus confesses the reason for this emotion: He is literally surrounded by sorrow (*perilupos*).

"Sit here." Keep awake with me, he asks his friends. What was Jesus asking them to watch for? Certainly it was not a request for a "lookout." Is this to be the final tribulation mentioned in chapter 24? Perhaps Jesus wanted them to be the first to witness God's power as God intervened to rectify the evil forces already set in motion.

For us the point is that in deep sorrow and serious trouble, Jesus draws his friends together and counsels prayer, waiting, and watching. He does not pace distractedly or rush headlong into rash, impractical, or inappropriate action.

In the sorrows and troubles of this life, we do well to follow his example, to gather quietly with our dear ones around a table prepared for our comfort. Here, together, we remain and are mindful of the strength we draw from each other and from his mystical "remaining," his presence here with us. And in these moments we pray together in the word of the great hymn by Horatius Bonar (1808-1889):

> Here, O my Lord, I see thee face to face;
> Here would I touch and handle things unseen;
> Here grasp with firmer hand eternal grace,
> And all my weariness upon thee lean.
>
> I have no help but thine; nor do I need
> Another arm save thine to lean upon;
> It is enough, my Lord, enough indeed;
> My strength is in thy might, thy might alone.

Matthew 26:39–41

³⁹And going a little farther he fell on his face and prayed, "My Father, if it be possible, let this cup pass from me; nevertheless, not as I will, but as thou wilt." ⁴⁰And he came to the disciples and found them sleeping; and he said to Peter, "So, could you not watch with me one hour? ⁴¹Watch and pray that you may not enter into temptation; the spirit indeed is willing, but the flesh is weak."

These few verses provide a terrifying picture of temptation. It is a testing on two levels: that of our Lord, and that of his disciples. The scene began at verse 36, "Jesus went with them to a place called Gethsemane." The place name itself ("place of the oil press") suggests crisis and pressure. Jesus does not abandon those who follow him. The Lord himself enters the place of testing with them.

We are not surprised to see the numbers dwindle drastically. The disciples are left behind. Peter, James, and John are left. Jesus alone falls on his face in the lowliest attitude of prayer. He addresses God in terms of intimacy: "Abba" (Papa, Daddy), "let this cup pass from me." This is no prayer of pietistic serenity; it is a plea in desperation, followed by a sigh of submission, "not as I will, but as thou wilt" (See Matt. 6:10,13). Having made this difficult decision, Jesus returns to his three dear friends for comfort—and finds them asleep.

By sleeping, Peter has already begun to betray the Christ he confessed. Jesus knows this, and, refraining from the anger that stress might well have justified, he gives Peter a word that he hopes will help in these troubled hours. And then he apologizes for Peter: You wanted to watch, but you were sleepy.

Watch.... Be wakeful.... Pray that you will not be tested. We recall these key phrases from the synoptic apocalypse (Mark 13, Matt. 24—25). But how much more powerful they are when we hear them in the midst of Jesus' own testing. For us, constant, vigilant prayer is necessary to be able to do his will. But that alone is not enough. As we reach up to God, God reaches down to us. As on that dark night Jesus provided Peter with a means to meet the test, so he provides us with a means today.

God reaches down and sets a table. It is his will that we gather there. We gather not for solace, but for strength. The spirit is still willing and the flesh is weak. God meets the need with spiritual food. As he would have us do, let us join him at Table.

Matthew 26:42-44

⁴² Again, for the second time, he went away and prayed, "My Father, if this cannot pass unless I drink it, thy will be done." ⁴³ And again he came and found them sleeping, for their eyes were heavy. ⁴⁴ So, leaving them again, he went away and prayed for the third time, saying the same words.

Jesus returns to prayer for the second and third times. The ordinal numbers in the Greek text serve to build emphasis and suspense. The intensity of Jesus' personal moment of crisis and decision is emphasized.

Special terms used in Greek show subtle differences in this passage. In verse 42 the conditional clauses ("if," *a*, a first class conditional assumed to be true, and "if not," *ean me*, a condition of the third class, undetermined) give us a window into Jesus' thought process and very real struggle. "If this cannot pass" (v. 42) shows more conviction that it, indeed, cannot be than "if it be possible, let this cup pass" (v. 39). "Thy will be done" (v. 42) is more emphatic than "not as I will, but as thou wilt" (v. 39).

Repetition and earnestness in prayer brings with it conviction about God's will and about what needs to be done in response to it.

The point is lost on Peter, James, and John. Even the evangelist seems embarrassed by their repeated lapses and adds the explanatory note that they slept because "their eyes were heavy" (v. 43). Three chances to support their Lord in prayer were frittered away.

Repetition can have two effects in our lives. It can dull by familiarity, or it can deepen by increased understanding. How do we respond to the frequent repetition of the Eucharist? Do we spiritually "nap" because it is so familiar to us? Or do we use it as an opportunity to penetrate more deeply into the mysteries of God and God's will for us? Both Jesus and his friends had to make decisions in this regard. And so do Jesus' disciples today.

Matthew 26:45–50

⁴⁵Then he came to the disciples and said to them, "Are you still sleeping and taking your rest? Behold, the hour is at hand, and the Son of man is betrayed into the hands of sinners. ⁴⁶Rise, let us be going; see, my betrayer is at hand."

⁴⁷While he was still speaking, Judas came, one of the twelve, and with him a great crowd with swords and clubs, from the chief priests and the elders of the people.

Matthew 26:45-50 37

⁴⁸"Now the betrayer had given them a sign, saying, "The one I shall kiss is the man; seize him." ⁴⁹And he came up to Jesus at once and said, "Hail, Master!" And he kissed him. ⁵⁰Jesus said to him, "Friend, why are you here?" Then they came up and laid hands on Jesus and seized him.

Jesus returns to his friends for the third time. He is resolved to do God's will. He finds them "still sleeping," and we hear behind his exclamation a warning: It is too late for spiritual preparation; I am now being betrayed. (See Matt. 24:36—25:13.) He says, "Arise, let us be going" for the disciples' sake. For Jesus, there is no escape.

Betrayed by his sleeping friends, who could not watch with him, Jesus faces the second betrayal of the evening. In the darkness, Judas arranges a signal so that the police force sent by the Sanhedrin can seize Jesus before his disciples have time to put up a fight. A kiss was a symbol of respect given by a pupil to a teacher. Ironically, Jesus' dignity is asserted as Judas salutes him, "Hail, Master!" Jesus responds to Judas with the word "Friend," companion.

The psalmist echoes the human situation here:

It is not an enemy who taunts me—
    then I could bear it;
It is not an adversary who deals insolently with me—
    then I could hide from him.
But it is you, my equal,
my companion, my familiar friend.
We used to hold sweet converse together;
within God's house we walked in fellowship.
                              (Ps. 55:12–14)

Unlike the psalmist, who calls down curses, Jesus is gentle with the friend who betrays him. Perhaps he sees in Judas the agent of God's will, which he has resolved to do.

It is a terrible thing to be betrayed by a friend. Many of us have suffered through this experience, even with those "within God's house." Because we have loved the betrayer, we cannot give way to the anger that would make the situation easier.

Jesus knows suffering. Sometimes he must feel about us as he felt about Judas. Are we by our thoughtlessness, our careless lack of attention to our Christian calling, betraying fellow Christians, betraying the Christ into the hands of sinners? As we do it to the least, we do it to him.

Whether we gather at the Table as betrayer or betrayed, Jesus loves us and wants to heal us. When we come to his Table, he addresses us as friends. "My body . . . for you." "My blood . . . for you."

> Come, ye disconsolate, where'er ye languish,
> Come to the mercy seat, fervently kneel!
> Here bring your wounded hearts,
> here tell your anguish:
> Earth has no sorrow that heaven cannot heal.
>
> Joy of the desolate, Light of the straying,
> Hope of the penitent, fadeless and pure!
> Here speaks the Comforter, tenderly saying,
> "Earth has no sorrow that heaven cannot cure."

(Thomas Moore, 1779–1852, and Thomas Hastings, 1784–1872)

Matthew 26:51-56

⁵¹And behold, one of those who were with Jesus stretched out his hand and drew his sword, and struck the slave of the high priest, and cut off his ear. ⁵²Then Jesus said to him, "Put your sword back into its place; for all who take the sword will perish by the sword. ⁵³Do you think that I cannot appeal to my Father, and he will at once send me more than twelve legions of angels? ⁵⁴But how then should the scriptures be fulfilled, that it must be so?" ⁵⁵At that hour Jesus said to the crowds, "Have you come out as against a robber, with swords and clubs to capture me? Day after day I sat in the temple teaching, and you did not seize me. ⁵⁶But all this has taken place, that the scriptures of the prophets might be fulfilled." Then all the disciples forsook him and fled.

In this scene we see in stark relief the two great sources of power in our world: physical (we might properly say "military") and spiritual.

From the betrayal of Judas, Matthew moves us immediately to the swordplay of the disciples. John's gospel tells us that Peter cut off the ear of Malchus, the high priest's slave (John 18:10). Jesus' words in verse 52 make it manifestly clear that a violent response to persecution is no better than betraying one's friends to persecution. In what is both a prediction and a prohibition, Jesus says that all who resort to violence will themselves become its victims. The end of military power, here represented by the sword, is an endless cycle of retaliation.

In the person of Jesus we see the result or the end of spiritual power. It maintains composure in the face of physical violence and even when it is deserted by friends and supporters. The physically powerful, if they are only that, will always be moral cowards. The Sanhedrin's secret police could not take Jesus in daylight in the temple because he was surrounded by followers. They had to make a raid on twelve men at night. The spiritually powerful are able by the will of God to transcend such violence.

The source of spiritual power is to be found in the fulfillment of God's will. In verse 56 Matthew puts the frequently used fulfillment formula in Jesus' own mouth. He is composed, at peace with his fate because he knows God's will is being done. Nothing can keep him from fulfilling God's will as revealed in scripture.

In the face of violence in our own lives—perhaps emotional violence, anger, hatred, resentment, prejudice, fear—we do well to remember Jesus' response to violence. We can sit down in peace at the Lord's Table because he overcame violence in himself and suffered it for our sakes. We see his body broken and his blood poured out. But its fruit in us is spiritual power to walk after Jesus' example in this life. He reminds us, "Blessed are the peacemakers" (Matt. 5:9).

Matthew 26:57–58

⁵⁷Then those who had seized Jesus led him to Caiaphas the high priest, where the scribes and the elders had gathered. ⁵⁸But Peter followed him at a distance, as far as the courtyard of the high priest, and going inside he sat with the guards to see the end.

What an unusual picture this is of Peter. Peter follows at a distance. Are we to see him as better than the other

Matthew 26:57-58

disciples? Is he perhaps waiting to see if there will be an opportunity to effect Jesus' release? At least, he follows along. Better, perhaps, but not good enough.

Peter is awaiting the outcome. Perhaps he does not want to commit himself too soon. If Jesus does call down legions of angels to rescue him, Peter will be there. If not, he can slip away into the crowd.

How often are we, like Peter, lurking around the edges of the action? It is human to want to see how a cause develops before we commit ourselves to it. The problem in the spiritual realm is that Jesus wants our commitment, no matter how desperate the situation looks. Jesus wants our testimony before the assembled judges pass down a ruling. When the verdict is in, it is too late for testimony.

As we gather together at his Table, some of us hang back. We watch at a distance. Perhaps we are waiting for the verdict. Perhaps a sense of our own shortcomings or failures restrains us.

George Herbert, the 17th century village pastor and poet, described our Lord's invitation to the hesitant soul as follows:

> Love bade me welcome; yet my soul drew back,
>   Guilty of dust and sin.
> But quick-eyed love, observing me grow slack
>   From my first entrance in,
> Drew nearer to me, sweetly questioning,
>   If I lacked anything.
>
> "A guest," I answered, "worthy to be here:"
>   Love said, "You shall be he."
> "I the unkind, ungrateful? Ah my dear,
>   I cannot look on Thee!"

Love took my hand, and smiling did reply,
> "Who made the eyes but I?"

"Truth, Lord; but I have marred them; let my shame
> Go where it doth deserve."
"And know you not," says Love, "who bore the
> blame?"
"My dear, then I will serve."
"You must sit down," says Love, "and taste my meat."
> So I did sit and eat.[15]

Do not hesitate to commit yourself to this Table. Love invites; Love welcomes you.

Matthew 26:59-60a

[59]Now the chief priests and the whole council sought false testimony against Jesus that they might put him to death, [60]but they found none, though many false witnesses came forward.

Few of us will face the opposition of a whole religious establishment. Jesus was opposed by the cultic, sacerdotal priesthood, by the educated lay leaders, and by the legal authorities of the Sanhedrin. In fact, these verses tell us that, in disregard of their own law, they actively sought persons who would lie about Jesus in public.

Unfortunately, there are always persons ready to rise in the world by stepping on others. Since the beginning of time, some have been willing to compromise honesty and integrity for what seems to be personal gain. Fortunately, a life of truth cannot be faulted by falsehoods. Even the most powerful men in ancient Israel were unable to find false testimony that would convict by religious law. Set before them was the Truth of God, incarnate.

We know how the story ended. Truth, apparently, did not win out. There was no "justice." For three days, falsehood "won." And then the situation looked very different, indeed. Acts tells us that many priests, those who opposed Jesus, came to believe in him (Acts 6:7). God prevented justice in order that mercy might reign.

The Table set before us symbolizes the one, pure, truthful act in all human history. The altar linens are white to symbolize this fact. Many will try to rise by dishonesty. One man chose to come down and suffer death for truth. And his life is the life that changed history, and his Table is the one that changes souls.

Matthew 26:60b-63

At last two came forward ⁶¹and said, "This fellow said,'I am able to destroy the temple of God, and to build it in three days.'" ⁶²And the high priest stood up and said, "Have you no answer to make? What is it that these men testify against you?" ⁶³But Jesus was silent. And the high priest said to him, "I adjure you by the living God, tell us if you are the Christ, the Son of God."

The best laid plots don't always work out as planned. After seeking false witnesses against Jesus, the chief priests and Sanhedrin finally turn up two men willing to distort Jesus' own words. Jesus had said, "Destroy this temple, and in three days I will raise it up" (John 2:19). He is not the one who destroys, but the One who raises up.

In their haste to bring false witness, the two men speak an ironic truth. God, indeed, has the power to destroy and to build, to lay down and to raise up. (See John 6:38-40, 45.) Then, as Matthew heaps irony upon irony, the high priest gives Jesus "equal time," an opportunity to refute the truth! Jesus says nothing. He cannot argue with what is true, and to attempt to explain himself would merely be to incriminate himself further in their eyes.

God alone breaks down to build up. This is as true of lives as of temples. Paul has taught us that our physical bodies are God's (1 Cor. 6:19). He bought us with a price: The temple was his Son's body.

And so the divine irony continues. We gather around this Table, a body of broken bones, and we are made whole by a body broken for our sakes. And his broken body and outpoured blood upbuild a new, spiritual body, the church. By his death, he did destroy the temple and its sacrificial system. He raised up a spiritual temple to serve God in holiness throughout eternity.

John's gospel assures us that no one robbed Jesus of his life. "I lay down my life that I may take it again" (John 10:17). Come, lay down your life and its brokenness at his Table, and he will give it back to you whole.

"He who eats my flesh and drinks my blood has eternal life, and I will raise him up at the last day" (John 6:54).

Matthew 26:63b-66

And the high priest said to him, "I adjure you by the living God, tell us if you are the Christ, the Son of God." "Jesus said to him, "You have said so. But I tell you,

hereafter you will see the Son of man seated at the right hand of Power, and coming on the clouds of heaven." ⁶⁵Then the high priest tore his robes, and said, "He has uttered blasphemy. "What is your judgment?" They answered, "He deserves death."

Nothing about our Lord's trial was routine. As he had actively sought false witnesses, now the high priest violates the law by addressing Jesus in a form that implies legal obligation to answer. He is, in effect, putting Jesus under oath.

But Jesus does not break his own prohibition against oaths (Matt. 5:33-37). He agrees with the high priest. Thus, in fact, he makes the high priest the "blasphemer." Then he adds an image from the prophet Daniel about the Son of man (Dan. 7:13). Interestingly, Jesus implies that the Son of man came down. That the "direction" is lost on the high priest is ironic. The Sanhedrin declares Jesus deserves death for agreeing with the high priest!

The high priest got it backwards. Even the accused tried to tell him. Jesus was not exalting himself, not "counting equality with God a thing to be grasped" (Phil. 2:6). He came down, took a humble form, served. For that reason, the eyes of faith see him at Table, the Host at a banquet for the redeemed. The power of God comes down in humble form, bread and wine, and the judgment meted out is "life." May the bread and wine, humble foods, served by the Hands of power, keep us in that life.

Matthew 26:67-68

⁶⁷Then they spat in his face, and struck him; and some slapped him, ⁶⁸saying, "Prophesy to us, you Christ! Who

is it that struck you?"

One of the most repulsive scenes in human history is enacted in these verses. (Have we seen so much television violence that its force is lost on us?) The priests and Sanhedrin heap guilt upon themselves by spitting in Jesus' face. Certainly there is no more degrading gesture! Mark records that Jesus was blindfolded (14:65), and this explains the mocking order that Jesus tell who it was that struck him. The church has read into this scene the words of Isaiah:

> I gave my back to the smiters,
>   and my cheeks to those who pulled out the beard;
> I hid not my face
>   from shame and spitting. (Isa. 50:6)

Gathered at his Table, we see the Man of Sorrows, despised, rejected, grieved. Leroy Lawson reminds us that sin "inflicts suffering on those least deserving of it. That is why it is up to the innocent to forgive. Only the injured one lifts the guilt of the injurer."[16]

Because Jesus silently bore undeserved suffering, we can be forgiven and delivered from guilt. The symbols on the Table are the seal of that deliverance. This cosmic truth is expressed in the choruses of Part II of Handel's great oratorio, *The Messiah*. "Surely He hath borne our griefs and carried our sorrows! He was wounded for our transgressions; He was bruised for our iniquities; the chastisement of our peace was upon Him. And with His stripes we are healed."

Matthew 26:69-75

⁶⁹Now Peter was sitting outside in the courtyard. And a maid came up to him, and said, "You also were with Jesus the Galilean." ⁷⁰But he denied it before them all, saying, "I do not know what you mean." ⁷¹And when he went out to the porch, another maid saw him, and she said to the bystanders, "This man was with Jesus of Nazareth." ⁷²And again he denied it with an oath, "I do not know the man." ⁷³After a little while the bystanders came up and said to Peter, "Certainly you are also one of them, for your accent betrays you." ⁷⁴Then he began to invoke a curse on himself and to swear, "I do not know the man." And immediately the cock crowed. ⁷⁵And Peter remembered the saying of Jesus, "Before the cock crows, you will deny me three times." And he went out and wept bitterly.

"This very night, before the cock crows, you will deny me three times" (Matt. 26:34). With this phrase Jesus had addressed Peter before asking him to watch and pray. Three times Peter is found asleep, and with no prayer to sustain him, three times Peter denied his Lord. Moreover, he forgets the Lord's prohibition against swearing and twice denies him with an oath (vs. 72, 74).

We usually think of this scene in relation to Peter. But what of the bystanders? Two servant girls recognize Peter. A crowd—well wishers of Jesus? the text doesn't say—suggests, on the basis of his accent, that Peter must have been with Jesus. We have no indication that these people meant Peter any harm. They were probably just the servants gathered for warmth and gossip. And yet Peter is so beside himself that he denies the truth.

God uses odd methods to call us to ourselves: serving girls, strangers in a crowd, a cock crowing. The question the scene poses for us as we gather at the Table is this: Would the bystanders of today recognize us as followers of the Galilean? Have they seen us walking with him in deeds of healing and humility and service? Would they recognize in our speech his wisdom and compassion? Would the way we talk give us away as belonging to him? Would we deny him with an oath and a curse?

This Table sustains our lives, but it also calls us to self-examination. For each of us a cock crows as a reminder of who and whose we are.

Matthew 27:1-2

When morning came, all the chief priests and the elders of the people took counsel against Jesus to put him to death; ²and they bound him and led him away and delivered him to Pilate the governor.

The Sanhedrin could not legally meet at night, so a dawn meeting was held to decide how to proceed. Since a capital sentence could not be handed down or carried out by the Sanhedrin (John 18:31), this meeting must have been held to discuss how best to get the Romans to consent to Jesus' execution. Since the work of a Roman official began at daybreak, Jesus must have been "handed over" or "delivered up" to Pilate shortly after dawn.

The Greek word we translate "delivered," *paredokan*, has an interesting history in our Lord's teaching. He uses it to mean both "entrusted" and "betrayed." When Jesus praises God for the "little ones" who hear and respond to his message, he affirms, "All things have been delivered [handed over] to me by my Father. . . .(Matt. 11:27). The same word is used in the parable of the talents when the master entrusts property to his servants (25:14-30). Thus, "to hand over" means "to entrust with."

It can also mean to betray. Jesus told the Twelve they would be handed over to councils and governments because of him (10:17-18). In predicting his Passion, he spoke of being "handed over" to men, to the chief priests, to teachers of the law (17:22-23; 20:18-19). Jesus will not be unfamiliar with the experiences his followers will have for his sake; he is the model for those who are to be "handed over."

At his memorial Table, we confront the two meanings of "handed over." We can examine and give ourselves to him, and partake worthily of the loaf and the cup. Or, by hasty, ill-considered, poorly prepared participation in the sacrament, we can betray the Lord again.

Paul reminds us to examine ourselves before we eat the bread and drink the cup. "For any one who eats and drinks without discerning the body eats and drinks judgment upon himself" (1 Cor. 11:29).

The Lord entrusts to us the tokens of his life and power. We dare not handle them carelessly. His bequest to us must not become our betrayal of him.

Matthew 27:3-5

³When Judas, his betrayer, saw that he was condemned, he repented and brought back the thirty pieces of silver to the chief priests and the elders, ⁴saying, "I have sinned in betraying innocent blood." They said, "What is that to us? See to it yourself." ⁵And throwing

down the pieces of silver in the temple, he departed; and he went and hanged himself.

By inserting the story of what happens to Judas, Matthew jumps ahead to the period after Jesus is condemned by Rome and the priests have returned to the temple to conduct the morning service. Judas, perhaps realizing that he has been duped in a plot much more serious than he had anticipated, is sorry for his conspiracy and attempts to return the blood money. But the priests and elders throw the blame for Jesus' conviction completely on Judas. Too late he knows he has betrayed his Lord and has not won the friendship of Jesus' persecutors by delivering him up to them.

To his credit, Judas returns the thirty pieces of silver. But the same weakness that led him to betray a friend causes him to despair and, according to Matthew, he dies by his own hand. In verse 3, Matthew reports Judas regretted his action, or was sorry, or, as the NIV translates, "he was seized with remorse." The Greek word *metamelomai* implies changing one's mind.

As we examine our hearts, we find ourselves confronted with a choice. We, like Judas, can live a life of regret. Or we can, as Jesus urges us from the beginning of his ministry, repent (Mark 1:15; Matt. 4:17). The word repent, *metanoia*, means a change of heart (in the ancient world the seat of the will and intelligence), a turning away from what came before. Had Judas repented of evil thoughts, he might have been spared regret.

Each time we share in the Lord's Table, we are offered not only a chance to repent, to turn away from sin and to begin anew, but we are given the strength and sustenance from these elements to do so. We are, in the words of the

Anglican service, "made clean by his body, and ... washed through his most precious blood."

Let us take a lesson from Judas' bitter experience and choose repentance over regret.

Matthew 27:6-10

⁶But the chief priests, taking the pieces of silver, said, "It is not lawful to put them into the treasury, since they are blood money." ⁷So they took counsel, and bought with them the potter's field, to bury strangers in. ⁸Therefore that field has been called the Field of Blood to this day. ⁹Then was fulfilled what had been spoken by the prophet Jeremiah, saying, "And they took the thirty pieces of silver, the price of him on whom a price had been set by some of the sons of Israel, ¹⁰and they gave them for the potter's field, as the Lord directed me."

Matthew singles out the chief priests apparently because Judas struck his bargain with them. It is telling that they have no apparent feeling for the suicide of a fellow human being. Judas' death means only that they are left with a legal problem. Only too glad to pay out blood money from the temple treasury, they are too scrupulous to put it back there. Writing some years later, Matthew gives the story an etiological thrust by accounting for an apparently well-known cemetery. In our own day, the idiom "potter's field" has come to mean a burial place for the poor and for strangers.

The fact that the prophecy quoted in verses 9-10 is closer to Zechariah 11:13 than to anything Jeremiah reported must not obscure Matthew's point. All that surrounds the events in Jesus' life is a fulfillment of scripture. Everything that happens is foreknown of God, and history moves toward God's appointed denouement.

Ironically enough, the events of Jesus' Passion have purchased another kind of "potter's field" for us. The outcast, the sinners, the poor, those estranged from God can be buried, free of charge, in the waters of baptism, washed in the blood of the Lamb, and rise from that grave to membership in Christ's own household. Buried strangers, we sit down together at a royal feast hosted by our Brother, a King.

Matthew 27: 11-14 (Compare John 18: 33-37)

¹¹Now Jesus stood before the governor; and the governor asked him, "Are you the King of the Jews?" Jesus said, "You have said so." ¹²But when he was accused by the chief priests and elders, he made no answer. ¹³Then Pilate said to him, "Do you not hear how many things they testify against you?" ¹⁴But he gave him no answer, not even to a single charge; so that the governor wondered greatly.

We have now moved back to the time of Jesus' trial before the Romans. Pilate (whose name is mentioned only once because Matthew wants to focus on Jesus) usually lived at the Roman headquarters city of Caesarea, but he was in Jerusalem during Passover to prevent disturbances.

While Pilate has lots of "evidence" against Jesus, he seemingly has trouble in his own mind convicting this man who was apparently so indifferent to the outcome of a capital sentence against him (See 27:18). Pilate asks, "Are you the King of the Jews?" It is unclear whether Pilate finds this an inflammatory title or has realized that the kingship in question is not a rival of Caesar's.

Jesus' answer, the same in all three synoptic accounts and in John, is literally translated, "You say" or, "You are saying." It is all Jesus speaks in his own defense. Jesus' silence echoes what Robert Gundry calls the "law of meekness" in Matthew: "Blessed are the meek, for they shall inherit the earth" (5:5, cf. 5:38-48).[17] Faced with the power of Rome, our Lord retains his composure.

Surely here the words of Isaiah are fulfilled:

As many were astonished at him—
his appearance was so marred, beyond human sem
   blance,
and his form beyond that of the sons of men—
so shall he startle many nations;
kings shall shut their mouths because of him;
for that which has not been told them they shall see,
and that which they have not heard they shall
   understand.

(Isa. 52:14-15)

One feels that Pilate, too, is silenced by this Jesus, this man who proves himself by who he is, not by what he says. Our Lord demonstrates clearly that sometimes silence is the most eloquent "utterance."

Gathered at his Table, we find the words of Isaiah to be the best gloss on this scene of Jesus' Passion. What they are not told, they will see; and what they have not heard, they will understand. Surely, the silent elements set before us, bread and wine, tell more of the truth of Jesus the Christ and God's great love than all the theological treatises ever written or all the sermons ever preached. Let us draw near and listen to his silence.

Matthew 27:15-18

[15] Now at the feast the governor was accustomed to release for the crowd any one prisoner whom they wanted. [16] And they had then a notorious prisoner, called Barabbas. [17] So when they had gathered, Pilate said to them, "Whom do you want me to release for you, Barabbas or Jesus who is called Christ?" [18] For he knew that it was out of envy that they had delivered him up.

Although the release of prisoners was characteristic of Roman festivals and the Panathenaic festival in Athens, the custom in Judea is not mentioned outside the gospels. Matthew here depends upon Mark, who may have inferred the custom from the Barabbas event. (Luke puts this incident after Jesus' visit to Herod. Cf. Luke 23:13-25.) While Mark and Luke say Barabbas was a murderer, from a Roman point of view his crime must not have been grave.

The implications of his name, however, are interesting. "Barabbas" literally translated is "son of a rabbi" or "son of a father." In several manuscripts, the text reads "Jesus called Barabbas."[18] The reading disappeared in early manuscripts because of the apparent reluctance of the early Christians to believe such a coincidence.

Realizing that envy is at the root of the charges against Jesus, Pilate takes an initiative for his release by calling for a public opinion poll or a popular vote. "Whom do you want me to release for you, Jesus called Barabbas or Jesus called the Christ?" We cannot help wondering whether, in the midst of the confusion of a milling crowd and the excitement of a religious festival with political overtones, the similarity of names led to a mistake. How well would a Roman governor have understood Aramaic? In any case, popular opinion has seldom been known as a source of considered and informed judgment.

At his Table another irony strikes us. Suppose Jesus had been released. How then would God have effected our redemption? The point is that our gracious God can bring good even from human errors of judgment and apparent confusion. Jesus chose to forgive even those who condemned him. And set before us are the tokens of that forgiveness. Let us partake with glad and grateful hearts.

Matthew 27:19-23

[19]Besides, while he was sitting on the judgment seat, his wife sent word to him, "Have nothing to do with that righteous man, for I have suffered much over him today in a dream." [20]Now the chief priests and the elders persuaded the people to ask for Barabbas and destroy Jesus. [21]The governor again said to them, "Which of the two do you want me to release for you?" And they said, "Barabbas." [22]Pilate said to them, "Then what shall I do with Jesus who is called Christ?" They all said, "Let him be crucified." [23]And he said, "Why, what evil has he done?" But they shouted all the more, "Let him be crucified."

Only Matthew records for us the message sent by

Claudia Procula who, according to tradition, was a proselyte. Perhaps in terms of Matthew's understanding of the Gentile mission, we are to see Pilate and Claudia as prototypical Gentile converts, Gentiles who see the goodness of Jesus.

However, while Pilate is engaged with messengers from his wife, the priests are employing themselves turning popular opinion against Jesus. The word "persuaded," *epeisan*, in verse 20 suggests the crowd is a victim of evil persuasion. Certainly, as he repeats verbatim the question from verse 17, Pilate must have felt the crowd would call for Jesus. Its persistent refusal to do so heightens the guilt of the prosecutors. The question is no longer one of justice or clemency; Pilate fears the frenzied mob.

We must stop to speculate about how often in history wrong decisions have been made on the basis of bad advice from the "authorities." How often have we been led astray by the desire to conform? The Nazi years in Germany provide an all too vivid and all too recent example of what happens when people listen uncritically to official forms of persuasion. Even in those dark years a few Christians resisted. Martin Niemöller, Corrie Ten Boom, Dietrich Bonhoeffer, the Confessing Church, and others had the courage to call for Jesus when all those around them shouted "Crucify!" and "Sieg Heil!"

When we come to the Table, we must come for strength as well as for solace. Each of us will have important choices to make in the days ahead. In the face of a system and of leaders who would persuade us to shout "Barabbas," would we have the courage to stand up for Jesus? May this holy meal strengthen us all to stand against popular opinion when it is evil and to stand for the things of God.

Matthew 27:24-26

²⁴"So when Pilate saw that he was gaining nothing, but rather that a riot was beginning, he took water and washed his hands before the crowd, saying, "I am innocent of this man's blood; see to it yourselves." ²⁵And all the people answered, "His blood be on us and on our children!" ²⁶Then he released for them Barabbas, and having scourged Jesus, delivered him to be crucified.

What scholars call the "Jewishness" of Matthew's gospel is evident in the hand washing scene, which only he records. Pilate employs a Jewish custom from Deuteronomy that all those present would recognize and understand (Deut. 21:1-9;. Compare Ps. 26:6). Pilate visually declares himself free from "innocent blood." He washes away responsibility for what depended upon him more than any other. Ironically, the term "innocent blood" is used only twice in the New Testament, in 27:4, when Judas Iscariot admits he has betrayed "innocent blood," and here as Pilate declares himself free of it.

Perhaps these confessions mean we are not to see Judas and Pilate as totally unredeemed. What we clearly do see are the cruel results of men who are unable to stand up to popular opinion or to official pressure. In this case, passive refusal to take the initiative to do good is as damning as the active call for evil, "His blood be on us and on our children." (Recall that Jewish law did hold perjurers accountable for false testimony that convicted innocent persons!) And so an innocent life is delivered up to the cruelty of scourging (which Josephus tells us was a preliminary to crucifixion and from which the victim often died) and death on a Roman cross. And Barabbas becomes the first man saved by Jesus' death.

In a cast of villains—weak, manipulated villains (Judas, Pilate, the crowd) and actively criminal villains (the Jewish authorities and Barabbas)—the innocent victim has triumphed. We gather not to memorialize the powerful, but the powerless. The Table is set to celebrate the One who "lost." God has "turned the tables." The Lamb triumphs over the lions of this world. May the words of the psalmist be our words as we gather at Table:

> Prove me, O LORD, and try me;
> > test my heart and my mind.
> For thy steadfast love is before my eyes,
> > and I walk in faithfulness to thee....
>
> I wash my hands in innocence,
> > and go about thy altar, O LORD,
> singing aloud a song of thanksgiving,
> > and telling all thy wondrous deeds.
> > > (Ps. 26: 2,3,6,7)

Matthew 27:27-31

²⁷Then the soldiers of the governor took Jesus into the praetorium, and they gathered the whole battalion before him. ²⁸And they stripped him and put a scarlet robe upon him, ²⁹and plaiting a crown of thorns they put it on his head, and put a reed in his right hand. And kneeling before him they mocked him, saying, "Hail, King of the Jews!" ³⁰And they spat upon him, and took

the reed and struck him on the head. ³¹And when they had mocked him, they stripped him of the robe, and put his own clothes on him, and led him away to crucify him.

The soldiers of the ancient world were not noted for refined sensibility or gentleness. As the Roman soldiers take Jesus to their quarters, they are leading him from "kangaroo court" to "kangaroo court."

Jesus suffers the indignity of being disrobed and dressed in a soldier's red cloak. The Peacemaker is dressed as a soldier. Given a false crown and scepter, the King of Kings and Lord of Lords is mocked. His silence in the face of abuse leads the soldiers to worse acts of violence. He is spat upon and beaten about the head. When the soldiers tire of the brutal game, they again strip Jesus, give him his own clothes and his own cross, and lead him out to Golgotha.

More ironic than the soldier's coat, the images of kingship, or the mocking tributes is the information that the soldiers were "kneeling before him." In a matter of hours, these same centurions confess, "Truly this was the Son of God!" (Matt. 27:54).

Any of the images of Jesus' Passion should drive us to our knees, but there is something especially poignant about this charade before the King of the Universe. Jesus allowed himself and the kingdom he proclaimed to be mocked in order that he might bestow citizenship in that very kingdom upon us who confess his name.

At his Table we fall to our knees, begging forgiveness for our sins, which continue to mock the lordship of Christ. And before we partake of the elements that cleanse our hearts we pray:

Forbid it, Lord, that I should boast,
Save in the death of Christ, my Lord;
All the vain things that charm me most,
I sacrifice them to His blood.

(Isaac Watts, 1674-1748)

Matthew 27:32

³²As they went out, they came upon a man of Cyrene, Simon by name; this man they compelled to carry his cross.

Simon, a Jew from the flourishing North African city of Cyrene, and the father of Alexander and Rufus, was, by the time the gospels were written, well known to the church at Rome (Mark 15:21; Rom. 16:13). Mark tells us that he was "coming out of the country," probably returning to the city from work in the fields. As he came in for Passover, he was pressed into service by the Romans and compelled to carry Jesus' cross.

Simon's feelings are not hard to imagine. He is tired from work and in no condition for more labor. He is angry about the Roman occupation of the land and the indignities afforded his conquered country. No doubt he is more than a little afraid for his own safety.

Simon may have taken up the cross reluctantly, but he bore it faithfully, and between the city gates and Golgotha he is converted by the very proximity to Jesus. We read in Acts 11:20 of a Cyrenean who preached to the Greeks about Jesus. Was this our Simon? From a man in a crowd forced by circumstance to carry a load, Simon is converted to a life of service.

God may very well lay burdens upon us to prepare us for service. But the negative circumstances of mortal life, the "slings and arrows of outrageous fortune" are not our cross. The cross is not something we passively endure; it is what we freely choose out of love for the Lord Jesus. The days of Roman occupation are over. Nobody can make us carry a cross. But at this Table the reminder set before us in flesh and blood may lead us to take up a cross for Christ's sake and for the gospel. And in carrying it, we, like Simon of Cyrene, may be transformed.

> Take up thy cross; let not its weight
> Fill thy weak spirit with alarm.
> His strength shall bear thy spirit up,
> And brace thy heart and nerve thine arm.
>
> Take up thy cross and follow Christ;
> Nor think till death to lay it down;
> For only one who bears the cross
> May hope to wear the glorious crown.
>
> *(Charles W. Everest, 1814-1877)*

Matthew 27:33-34

[33] And when they came to a place called Golgotha (which means the place of the skull), [34] they offered him wine to drink, mingled with gall; but when he tasted it, he would not drink it.

The "bitter wine" is a feature that is common to all the accounts of Jesus' Passion. Sometimes it appears as it is offered on a sponge (Mark 15:36; John 19:29). In Luke it is part of the soldiers' mockery to offer Jesus "vinegar," to give the king cheap wine (Luke 23:36-37) What was wine doing here at Calvary? [19] Why an image of feasting at the place of death?

Perhaps the Roman soldiers brought it along, as we know it was their custom to drink wine mingled with myrrh. Many believe it was a narcotic offered to ease pain. It has even been suggested that the wealthy women of Jerusalem provided this offering of mercy to fulfill the requirements of Proverbs 31:6: "Give strong drink to him who is perishing, and wine to those in bitter distress."

Whatever its origin, we note that Jesus does not take the wine. He has told the disciples at the Last Supper, "I tell you I shall not drink again of this fruit of the vine until that day when I drink it new with you in my Father's kingdom" (Matt. 26:29). Jesus remains faithful to his promises.

When, at the Lord's Table, we have reflected upon this "bitter wine," we have usually associated it with the cup of suffering that our Lord endured for us. Or, quite rightly, we have understood it to be the wine of his spilled blood. Here in Matthew, however, we see another possibility, another layer of meaning. Perhaps the wine mingled with gall is an image of compassion in a dark and devilish place. Perhaps it represents the fact that someone had foresight and compassion on sufferers.

Set on the Table are emblems that assure us we have been considered and provided for. No suffering we might endure is above God's power to ease it. "Earth has no sorrow that heaven cannot cure." The wine set before us, the very lifeblood of Jesus, is the proof of his compassion for us. It is vivid testimony that God's mercy has provided for our sustenance and that God's Son has redeemed all the dark circumstances of our lives.

Matthew 27:35-37[20]

³⁵And when they had crucified him, they divided his garments among them by casting lots; ³⁶then they sat down and kept watch over him there. ³⁷And over his head they put the charge against him, which read, "This is Jesus the King of the Jews."

After Jesus is nailed to the cross, the soldiers gamble for his clothing. (See Ps. 22:18.) Part of the customary pay of the executioners in the Roman world was the victim's clothes. John tells us that Jesus' undergarment was seamless, and so special lots were cast for that piece (John 19:23-24). Matthew carefully records that the soldiers remained to watch or to guard the dying criminals. He wants to forestall any rumors that Jesus was removed from the cross while still alive.

As was customary, the condemned criminals carried signs stating the nature of their crimes. These signs were then affixed to their crosses. The charge Pilate assigns to Jesus is "King of the Jews." Perhaps Pilate uses the charge as a chance to sneer at the Jews. Or perhaps, since he insists that this title remain, he, too, confesses the Christ in his own terrible way. (See John 19:19-22.)

John further records that the sign was written in Hebrew, Latin, and Greek, the three major languages of the ancient world. No people or national group is excluded from knowledge of the charge: "This is Jesus, the

King of the Jews." From the universality of a criminal accusation, the church has expanded to become universal. People of every race and tongue now claim Jesus as their king.

As we gather at the Table, we remember that this feast is enacted in thousands of places this day. Our Lord is remembered and praised in hundreds of languages. May this feast be for us a symbol of the universality of the church, and may we resolve to do the work of evangelism until every race and nation confesses that Christ is Lord, to the glory of God.

Matthew 27: 38-40

³⁸Then two robbers were crucified with him, one on the right and one on the left. ³⁹And those who passed by derided him, wagging their heads ⁴⁰and saying, "You who would destroy the temple and build it in three days, save yourself! If you are the Son of God, come down from the cross."

With verse 39, Matthew begins to describe the parade of those who pass by Jesus to mock and hurl insults. (See Ps. 22:8.) The first group is simply "those who pass by," *paraporeuomenoi*. People walking to and from Jerusalem pause to taunt the tortured Jesus. Not unlike many persons casually connected to major decisions, they do not have their facts straight. They cling to the slander of the trial that accused Jesus of blaspheming against the temple. This, as we know, is a misrepresentation of what Jesus actually said. (See Matt. 26:59-61; 24:1-2.)

How often are we quick to judge a situation by hearsay or by casual observation? Do we cling to rumor or ferret out the truth? Are we the "head-waggers" of our own day?

Perhaps the next time we are tempted to jeer or deride, this scene of the Passion will pass before us. How much it must have heightened Jesus' agony to be unjustly mocked! And what if he had "come down from the cross"? Who, then would have sealed our pardon in blood?

The Lord's Table can be for us a table of resolve, an altar at which we re-covenant ourselves and our motives to God. Let us resolve to become more inquiring and less judgmental.

Matthew 27:41-43

⁴¹"So also the chief priests, with the scribes and elders, mocked him, saying, ⁴²"He saved others; he cannot save himself. He is the King of Israel; let him come down now from the cross, and we will believe in him. ⁴³He trusts in God; let God deliver him now, if he desires him; for he said,'I am the Son of God.'"

The next group of mockers are the priests, scribes, and elders who precipitated the whole gory sacrifice. While it is unlikely that such persons would have been on Golgotha at Passover time, Matthew's notation that they are here serves to intensify Jesus' suffering by underlining his separation and rejection from his own people and religious heritage. Their taunts, "If you are the Christ, the Son of God..." echo the very words of Satan to Jesus in the wilderness. (See Matt. 4:3,6; Wisdom 2:6-20.)

The irony is, of course, that Jesus' enemies speak the truth. They taunt, "If God loved, God would save." This is exactly what God is doing. Jesus is saving others. The priests, scribes, and those educated in the law have not understood the point of the reversals that Jesus proclaimed would characterize the kingdom of God. The mighty will be put down. The last will be first. The servant will be the leader. He who suffers and dies will be he who saves.

Satan was right. Jesus could have called down legions of angels to rescue him. But by an act of will, he chose to die. Had he saved himself, humanity would have been lost. This is the act of love we commemorate with bread and wine. This is the selflessness to which we are called in the fellowship of his Table.

Matthew 27:38 and 44

³⁸Then two robbers were crucified with him, one on the right and one on the left.... ⁴⁴And the robbers who were crucified with him also reviled him in the same way.

Finally, the robbers crucified with Jesus "reviled him in the same way." Matthew's characteristic use of *kai* to mean "even" makes them the most despicable in the list of mockers. Even transgressors with whom Jesus was numbered, whose sins he was bearing (Isa. 53:12), taunted him.

The word translated "robbers," *lastai*, may also mean "revolutionary," in which case these men may have been in league with Barabbas, so that Jesus' conviction hastened their own death.

Luke's expansion of this incident softens it somewhat. One criminal taunts Jesus; the other defends the Lord's innocence and begs for his mercy. Compassionate even in his own agony, Jesus promises, "Today you will be with me in Paradise" (Luke 23:39-43).

Here, at the cross, at the bitter end of his life, Jesus shows us that it is "never too late." As long as we have breath, the possibility remains that we can confess Jesus as Christ and join him in Paradise. The sophistication of theology may argue against "deathbed" or "foxhole" confessions, but certainly, as the thief on the cross dramatically shows, it is better than no change of heart at all. Earl Marlatt's hymn poses the crucial question for us:

"Are you able" to remember,
When a thief lifts up his eyes,
That his pardoned soul is worthy
Of a place in Paradise?

(Earl Marlatt, 1892-   )

Matthew 27:45

⁴⁵Now from the sixth hour there was darkness over all the land until the ninth hour.

The sixth hour of the day is noon; the ninth hour is 3 o'clock p.m., the period of time when, in the Mediterranean world, the sun should be high. For the pagans and Roman soldiers in Jerusalem, a darkness at noon would have been the portent of the death of a great person.

Both the prophets Amos and Jeremiah speak of catastrophe under the figure of darkness at noon. In a scene of punishment of Jerusalem, Jeremiah describes the sun going down while it is day (Jer. 15:9). Amos describes God's displeasure:

> "And on that day . . .
> I will make the sun go down at noon,
> and darken the earth in broad daylight" (Amos 8:9).

The darkness over the earth is no mere eclipse; it is a sign of God's wrath. John's gospel illuminates the symbolism of the scene even more. There Jesus announces, "I am the light of the world; he who follows me will not walk in darkness, but will have the light of life" (John 8:12). As long as Jesus is in the world, he is the light of the world (John 9:5). Now, as the light of life is about to be extinguished by sinful men, the world is shrouded in a cosmic darkness. Just as it is dark (night) when Judas goes out to betray Jesus (John 13:30), so it is dark when Jesus is "forsaken" by God.

This is not the end of the story. "God is light and in him is no darkness at all" (1 John 1:5). The shrouded gloom of Good Friday is utterly and forever dispersed by the brilliant light shining forth from the empty tomb on the first day of the week. We gather this first day of each week to commemorate the saving act of our Lord. The action that assures us of salvation is most clearly set before us on the table in the form of bread and wine. Each time the bread is broken and the cup is poured out, we reaffirm with thanksgiving, "The light shines in the darkness, and the darkness has not overcome it" (John 1:5).

Matthew 27:46

"And about the ninth hour Jesus cried with a loud voice, "Eli, Eli, lama sabachthani?" that is, "My God, my God, why hast thou forsaken me?"

No cry in history is more heartrending than the final words of Jesus, which Matthew retains in their original Aramaic and then translates into Greek for his readers.

As he bore the sins of humanity, Jesus experienced the chief bitterness of his death as the apparent forsaking by God. He expresses his feelings in what may be a quotation from Psalm 22:1, the "anguished prayer of David as a godly sufferer victimized by the vicious and prolonged attacks of enemies whom he has not provoked and from whom the Lord has not (yet) delivered him. . . . They [the evangelists] saw in the passion of Jesus the fulfillment of the cry of the righteous sufferer."[21]

In its course, Psalm 22 becomes a song of praise for God's deliverance. Scholars dispute, therefore, whether we should see this cry of Jesus from the cross as a cry of desolation and loss, or as the prayer of a righteous sufferer who is to be victorious. It is an issue not easily resolved.

The cry of Jesus from the cross points to our dilemma at his table. Are we to hold somber vigil for his suffering or to rejoice and celebrate his victory? Both moods are appropriate, and both are to be expected, for they reflect the complexity and reality of our lives. We have our moments of defeat and of triumph, and both are appropriately carried to this Table. We break bread and drink wine for solace and strength and also with "glad and generous hearts" (Acts 2:46). In whatever state we find ourselves, his Table provides a proper place setting for us and assures us of his "favor and goodness towards us; and that we are very members incorporate in the mystical body of [his] Son, the blessed company of all faithful people; and ... heirs, through hope, of [his] everlasting kingdom."[22]

Matthew 27:47-49[23]

[47]And some of the bystanders hearing it said, "This man is calling Elijah." [48]And one of them at once ran and took a sponge, filled it with vinegar, and put it on a reed, and gave it to him to drink. [49]But the others said, "Wait, let us see whether Elijah will come to save him."

Apparently in the shuffle around the crucifixion site when Jesus calls out, "*Eli, Eli . . . ,*" the bystanders hear the name of the prophet Elijah. The story of Elijah's departure is told in 2 Kings 2:9-12. Elijah did not die but was taken up to heaven alive. According to well-known Jewish tradition, he would return in times of distress and rescue the righteous. It was thus not surprising to think that Jesus might be calling Elijah.

What the mockers at the foot of the cross could not see was that One greater than Elijah was working to save. Jesus remained on the cross to rescue us. His salvation is represented before us in bread and wine. And we do not need to wait to see if it will save. Week by week we experience its effect among us as we are renewed and strengthened for service. Jesus comes to us in this holy sacrament, renewing within us the seeds of righteousness. May we be worthy fruit for his harvest.

Matthew 27:48

⁴⁸And one of them at once ran and took a sponge, filled it with vinegar, and put it on a reed, and gave it to him to drink.

John's gospel tells us that twice Jesus calls out in thirst (John 19:28-29). The sour wine, *oxous*, was a favorite drink of the lower classes. Perhaps we have here another instance of Matthew's concern to show how Jesus' life and death fulfills the Old Testament.

> They gave me poison for food,
> and for my thirst they gave me vinegar to drink.
> (Ps. 69:21)

In the *Gospel of Peter*, a fragment of a Passion narrative, the drink is understood to have caused premature death:

> And one of them said, Give him to drink gall with vinegar: and they mingled it and gave him to drink: and they fulfilled all things and accomplished their sins upon their own heads. (vs. 16-17)[24]

It is also possible to see in this anonymous person's rush to offer Jesus a drink a kind attempt to assuage his thirst. But Jesus takes no wine, having promised to abstain until he drinks it new with his disciples in the kingdom (Matt. 26:29).

Before us is a foretaste of that banquet in the kingdom. Jesus comes to sup with us at table. May this image of anonymous kindness—Jesus offered a drink in his final agony—remind us of our responsibility to help those in distress. As we accept the wine from the hand of the Lord, may we be strengthened for action in the world on his behalf.

Matthew 27:50

⁵⁰And Jesus cried again with a loud voice and yielded up his spirit.

Having called out to God (27:46), Jesus cries out one more time. Luke records his words, "Father, into thy hands I commit my spirit!" (Luke 23:46).

Throughout Matthew, Jesus, the great teacher who fulfills Israel's hopes, is a majestic figure. Here, in his last moments, he is depicted by Matthew as dying of his own accord. He "yielded up his spirit." The Greek *apheken* means to let go or to send away. Jesus returns his life to its source in God. His physical body used up, the spirit returns to its Creator.

As Paul so beautifully explains in 1 Corinthians 15, God gives a body as God chooses: the physical first and then the spiritual. When the physical is discarded, God stands ready to receive the spirit. As Jesus was a "man of dust," he returns to be a "man of heaven" (1 Cor. 15:48-49).

As Jesus' physical body was sustained by food—fish, bread, wine—so are our earthly bodies sustained. But the Lord's Supper is a meal for the sustenance of the spiritual body, a means to maintain our imperishable spirits.

On the cross, Jesus gave his spirit to God. In this meal, he gives a measure of that spirit to us. We remember both gifts, and we wait for the day when "the trumpet will sound ... and we shall be changed" (1 Cor. 15:52). In the words of Bernard of Clairvaux (1091-1153):

> Jesus, the very thought of Thee
> With sweetness fills my breast;
> But sweeter far Thy face to see,
> And in Thy presence rest.

Matthew 27:51a

51 And behold, the curtain of the temple was torn in two, from top to bottom; ...

Romantic literature of the nineteenth century often relied on the supposed sympathy of the natural world to human events. Something like this is at work here. To convey the import of Jesus' death and to portray his deity, Matthew reaches back to the Old Testament and to the prophets for images of God's power and of new beginnings: the torn curtain, the earthquake, and the raising of the saints.

Most commentators assume the "curtain of the temple" was the partition separating the Holy of Holies from all but the high priests of Judaism. The writer of the Letter to the Hebrews describes it as follows: "... but into the second only the high priest goes, and he but once a year, and not without taking blood which he offers for himself and for the errors of the people. By this the Holy Spirit indicates that the way into the sanctuary is not yet opened ... " (Heb. 9:7-8).

The rending of the temple curtain at the moment of Jesus' death signals the end of the temple cult. There is no longer a need for sacrifice. Through his blood, Christ secured "an eternal redemption" (Heb. 9:12).

From another perspective, the rent curtain symbolizes that the barrier between humans and God has been removed. We all have direct access to the Holy of Holies through the blood of Jesus. In the words of the beautiful hymn by Horatius Bonar (1808-1889), "Here, O my Lord, I see thee face to face." The way into holiness is open to us all.

"For Christ, our paschal lamb, has been sacrificed. Let us, therefore, celebrate the festival . . . " (1 Cor. 5:7-8) and celebrate the fact that free access to God has been made available to us through Jesus.

Matthew 27:51b-53

. . . and the earth shook, and the rocks were split; ⁵² the tombs also were opened, and many bodies of the saints who had fallen asleep were raised, ⁵³ and coming out of the tombs after his resurrection they went into the holy city and appeared to many.

The details of the opening of the tombs are mentioned by Matthew alone. Matthew includes this event because it reflects the expectations of the Jews. Eschatalogical literature of Israel describes a time when the Mount of Olives will split into two parts, and the dead will rise from the two halves. (See Zech. 14:4.) This glorious resurrection of the just was expected as one of the signs of the end.

Through the prophet Ezekiel the Lord has spoken:

Behold, I will open your graves, and raise you from your graves, O my people; and I will bring you home into the land of Israel. And you shall know that I am the LORD, when I open your graves, and raise you from your graves, O my people. And I will put my Spirit within you, and you shall live . . . (Ezek. 37:12-14; cf. Dan. 12:2).

Matthew looks ahead to the resurrection of Jesus as he describes how the saints also made "resurrection appearances" in the "holy city" (a term for Jerusalem used only in Matthew). (See also 1 Cor. 15:20; Col. 1:18; Rev. 1:5). The point is that, with Jesus, the general resurrection has begun, and the power of death is vanquished.

Here is the heart of the Christian message: Jesus has conquered death. The term "gospel" means "good news of a victory." We gather at his Table for a victory celebration. The somber and terrible scenes of the passion must never obscure the light and joy of resurrection. Our song of celebration is that "Death is swallowed up in victory" and our grace before this meal is, "Thanks be to God who gives us the victory through our Lord Jesus Christ" (1 Cor. 15:54, 57).

Matthew 27:54

⁵⁴**When the centurion and those who were with him, keeping watch over Jesus, saw the earthquake and what took place, they were filled with awe, and said, "Truly this was the Son of God!"**

The Roman soldiers who presided over the crucifixion of criminals had seen firsthand the behavior of Jesus and his followers in these grim circumstances. They had witnessed the marvelous signs in nature when Jesus "gave up his spirit." On the basis of what they had seen, they confessed, "This was the Son of God."

Oddly enough, the scene hearkens back to the magi, the Oriental sages who worshiped Jesus before his own people recognized him (Matt. 2:1-12). The magi and the centurions are the vanguard Gentiles in the church, the model for non-Jews who were to accept Jesus as Messiah. On the basis of what they see, they confess. (The confession here is the object of scholarly comment because "Son of God" has no definite article and might thus be rendered, "This man was a son of God.")

In the crisis circumstances of life—in tragedy, disaster, suffering—would those who observed our actions be led to remark, " He was a son of God" or "She was a daughter of God"? Even callous Roman soldiers, inured to torture and death, were moved by Jesus' last moments. In this, as in all things, he sets an example for us.

As we sit down at his Table, may we make it our intention to be more Christlike. We pray that strangers and the spiritually hardened and dying may see our witness and confess, "Truly they are children of God." Let us as children approach the Table.

Matthew 27:55-56

[55]There were also many women there, looking on from afar, who had followed Jesus from Galilee, ministering to him; [56]among them were Mary Magdalene, and Mary the mother of James and Joseph, and the mother of the sons of Zebedee.

Matthew 27:55-56 77

Many women followed Jesus, drawn to a rabbi who gave them equal status in the spiritual community. Luke's gospel stresses the ministry of faithful women who joined Jesus' disciples in Galilee and followed, providing for them "out of their means" (Luke 8:1-3). In Matthew, these women give the Passion story continuity, and their presence at Jesus' death makes them reliable witnesses to his resurrection (cf. chap. 28). Here, however, they are simply "looking on from afar" (v. 55).

Sometimes all we can do is stand by and watch. Sometimes silent vigil is the ministry to which God calls us. John Milton's sonnet titled "When I Consider How My Light Is Spent" comes to mind:

> . . . God doth not need
> Either man's work or his own gifts, who best
> Bear his milde yoak, they serve him best. His State
> Is Kingly. Thousands at his bidding speed
> And post o'er Land and Ocean without rest:
> They also serve who only stand and waite.

We cannot know how much comfort may be derived from our simple presence in situations of anguish, pain, and sorrow. Sometimes being there, being present, is all that is called for.

As the faithful women served by standing looking on, as we serve by our presence, so the Table of the Lord—a constant source of strength and comfort—"stands and waits," stands ready to receive, waits with infinite patience for each one to come. In the words of the hymn by Will L. Thompson (1847-1909), "Softly and Tenderly,"

"Patiently Jesus is waiting and watching, Watching for you and for me."

His presence here is real. His invitation is to all who call him Lord.

Matthew 27:57-60

⁵⁷When it was evening, there came a rich man from Arimathea, named Joseph, who also was a disciple of Jesus. ⁵⁸He went to Pilate and asked for the body of Jesus. Then Pilate ordered it to be given to him. ⁵⁹And Joseph took the body, and wrapped it in a clean linen shroud, ⁶⁰and laid it in his own new tomb, which he had hewn in the rock; and he rolled a great stone to the door of the tomb, and departed.

The memory of Joseph of Arimathea is venerated with good reason. A wealthy man and an observant Jew from a village twenty two miles northwest of Jerusalem, Joseph had every reason to absent himself from the Jesus situation. And yet he chose to become involved.

It was customary to leave the bodies of crucified criminals on their crosses until they decayed or were eaten by birds or animals. Dead bodies, especially those of criminals, were considered unclean, and the law forbade the use of a new tomb again if a criminal were placed in it.

Joseph risked the wrath of the Roman occupation when he went to Pilate to ask for the body of Jesus. (Unless Jesus were really dead, Pilate could not release the corpse. Thus the death of Jesus is established.) He made himself ritually unclean during the highest holy days when he wrapped the body in "a clean linen shroud." He lost the use of his tomb (which Mark suggests he may have hewn from the rock himself, Mark 15:46) when he placed Jesus' body there. This rich man in town for Passover himself rolls the great stone over the door of the tomb. And then he departs, and we never hear of him again.

Joseph of Arimathea understood the parable of the good Samaritan, who stopped and became involved when others (for "good" religious and political reasons) passed by. And like that Samaritan, he knew when to leave. He finished what he set out to do, and departed.

In this action, Joseph is like Jesus, who, forsaking his high standing, came down and became involved in human need and, having finished what he set out to do, departed. But Jesus left us souvenirs of his visit: a towel and a basin, the symbols of humble service; the loaf and the cup, the symbols of great love. May the bread and wine strengthen and encourage us to become like Joseph of Arimathea, to dare to become involved in human need.

Matthew 27:60b-61

... and he rolled a great stone to the door of the tomb, and departed. ⁶¹Mary Magdalene and the other Mary were there, sitting opposite the sepulchre.

The women who have followed Jesus from Galilee never desert him. They stood in vigil at the cross, and now they have followed the man who took their Lord's body (perhaps he was a stranger to them) to see that needful attention is paid. By again calling attention to the women, Matthew makes sure the reader knows that there was constant watch over what took place. There can be no mistake about what transpired. A great stone seals the tomb, and the women sit in silent vigil, representing the care for the persecuted that discipleship requires.

Today, other mothers stand in silent vigil. Every day on the Plaza de Mayo in the capital city of Argentina, women stand in silent vigil of protest. Their children and husbands have been seized and held without trial and are now officially reported as "missing." The mothers stand and wait, serving as a reminder to all that the innocent have been wrongly treated.

How eloquent such silence can be! Set silently before us are bread and wine, symbols of another innocent Victim. Our hearts wait for the reception of his body and blood, and we, too, await the day when the captives will be released and the dead raised. We wait beside the tomb, but, for us, the stone is already rolled away.

> Sit at the feast, dear Lord,
> Break Thou the bread;
> Fill Thou the cup that brings
> Life to the dead;
> That we may find in Thee
> Pardon and peace;
> And from all bondage win
> A full release.
>
> (May P. Hoyt)

Matthew 27:62-66

⁶²Next day, that is, after the day of Preparation, the chief priests and the Pharisees gathered before Pilate

⁶³and said, "Sir, we remember how that imposter said, while he was still alive, 'After three days I will rise again.' ⁶⁴Therefore order the sepulchre to be made secure until the third day, lest his disciples go and steal him away, and tell the people, 'He has risen from the dead,' and the last fraud will be worse than the first." ⁶⁵Pilate said to them, "You have a guard of soldiers; go, make it as secure as you can." ⁶⁶So they went and made the sepulchre secure by sealing the stone and setting a guard.

Peculiar to Matthew, this scene may represent his access to a Jerusalem tradition. It presupposes that the tomb was found to be empty, or there would have been no reason for its inclusion. It prepares us for Matthew 28:11-15.

While Jesus' friends rested on the Sabbath, the Pharisees worked, apparently having found another legal loophole that allowed them to do so. Jesus' enemies are apparently more apprehensive about his resurrection than his friends, and so they go to make sure the tomb is secure. Once again enlisting Roman help, the Jewish officials call Pilate "Lord," the title we reserve for Jesus. Characteristically, Pilate responds ambiguously. He either gives them a Roman guard or suggests they already have the temple guard (v. 65).

What the Jewish leaders fear is that Jesus' disciples will spread the rumor that he has risen, and "the last fraud will be worse than the first" (v. 64). To them the first "fraud" was Jesus' claim to be Messiah; the second would be his rising from the dead.

Of course, we know that Jesus was not a fraud. He was and is who he claimed to be. His death and resurrection was no trick accomplished by stealth. He died, was buried, and rose exactly as he had said he would (Matt. 16:21). Jesus' truthfulness, and this fact of history, mean we can trust his words to us.

As we sit at his Table, let us reflect on his great faithfulness. All he promises is accomplished in God's good time. Thus let us look forward in hope to the future and the promised day when we shall drink with him anew in the Father's kingdom.

Matthew 28:1-4

Now after the sabbath, toward the dawn of the first day of the week, Mary Magdalene and the other Mary went to see the sepulchre. ²And behold, there was a great earthquake; for an angel of the Lord descended from heaven and came and rolled back the stone, and sat upon it. ³His appearance was like lightning, and his raiment white as snow. ⁴And for fear of him the guards trembled and became like dead men.

The time of day in this section of the story is problematic. "After the Sabbath" would be after sunset on Saturday. Yet Matthew says the women came "toward dawn," that is, when it was not yet light. Whenever the exact time, the women risk the danger of coming alone in the darkness of night to continue their silent vigil. In Matthew, they bring no spices because they think the tomb is sealed. What a surprise awaits them!

In the darkness, the great light of the angel is more dramatic. There has been an earthquake and the stone is rolled away. The guards are "petrified," frozen with fear, become "like dead men" (v. 4). What an ironic reversal that is! The living who were to guard the dead seem dead themselves.

Certainly the focal person in the scene is the dazzling angel of the Lord. We have met him before in Matthew in the infancy narratives, where he appears to Joseph to explain the precise meaning of events and to assign definite tasks (Matt. 1:20, 24; 2:13, 19). And those are his functions here.

The women come out of love to watch and to wait. The glorious angel comes to explain God's work. The soldiers who came because of the religious leaders' fear, are frozen with fear. Aren't these the cast of characters in our enactment of the Lord's Supper?

Some come because others have made them do so and are so spiritually deadened that the presence of the Lord does not raise them. Some come in love and reverence to await the message God gives in bread and wine. And the shining angel hovers at the Table to inspire and to assign a task.

On the first day of the week, our cast of characters are assembled. May we hear the message of the angels. And may the spiritually dead hear the words of the ancient Christian hymn,

"Awake, O sleeper, and arise from the dead,
and Christ shall give you light" (Eph. 5:14).

Matthew 28:5-7

⁵But the angel said to the women, "Do not be afraid; for I know that you seek Jesus who was crucified. ⁶He is not here; for he has risen, as he said. Come, see the place

where he lay. ⁷Then go quickly and tell his disciples that he has risen from the dead, and behold, he is going before you to Galilee; there you will see him. Lo, I have told you."

If seasoned soldiers of the Roman Empire were frozen with fear at the sight of the angel, imagine the state of the simple Galilean women! The angel's word to them, to those who have come on a mission of love and service, is "Do not be afraid."

The Jesus whose body they have come to see is risen "as he said." Three times Jesus told his followers what would happen (16:21; 17:23; 20:19) and now, as the empty tomb and the folded grave clothes bear witness (John 20:7), it has happened as he said.

Now Jesus will go before them into Galilee, also as he said (26:32). Jesus leads as a shepherd leads his flock, and, as has been the case in Matthew's gospel, disciples follow. After Passover it would have been natural for them to return to their homes in Galilee, to return to the daily round of ordinary activity. The angel asserts, "*There* you will see him."

"Don't fear," "Go tell," "There you will see him." The messages of the angel are messages for all time. We all need something to go before, to lead us in daily life. We have a message to proclaim about our risen Leader: We meet him in the ordinary circumstances of life.

Ordinary things: bread and wine. Here we see him. Set before us on the Table are tokens of an outrageous promise given to simple women by an angelic messenger: He is risen and goes before you, and you will see him. As Fred Craddock has written in another context, ". . . the church has continued to experience the presence . . . in the table fellowship."[25]

He is risen. He has gone and is going before us. And in the breaking of bread and outpouring of wine, here, in our own hometown, we do see him as he promised.

Matthew 28:8

[8]So they departed quickly from the tomb with fear and great joy, and ran to tell his disciples.

Fear and great joy characterize the events surrounding the resurrection. Those who crucified him and complied in the deed have every reason to fear. Those who followed and believed in his promises have every reason to rejoice. And every mixture and shade of these emotions is appropriate to this moment.

Just as the angel casts us back to the infancy narrative, so the great joy of the women reminds us of the magi: "When they saw the star, they rejoiced exceedingly with great joy" (Matt. 2:10). Both the women and the magi respond to what they have seen, to a manifestation of God's power and presence. When the magi returned to their own country, and when the women ran to tell the disciples, their reports were on the basis of what they, personally, had experienced.

The theme of Matthew 28 is "go tell." And the subject of the message is always that which has been experienced: an angelic visitation, an empty tomb, the risen Jesus. These are matters of great joy.

Christianity does not ask us to live impossibly good lives on the basis of a set of theories or principles. It asks us to respond in love to what we have seen and experienced. Our lives are full of angelic messages and empty tombs, fears that prove unfounded, and it is of this that we must "go tell."

We experience in the meal on the Lord's Table the power of his love and the joy of his empty tomb. We may come in fear, but we leave in joy. As you leave his Table, he gives you a commission: Who should you go and tell? Having experienced this love in bread and wine, broken and poured out, you, too, have a message to share, a message based on your experience of empty tombs and holy Tables.

Matthew 28:9-10

⁹And behold, Jesus met them and said, "Hail!" And they came up and took hold of his feet and worshiped him. ¹⁰Then Jesus said to them, "Do not be afraid; go and tell my brethren to go to Galilee, and there they will see me."

When Jesus meets the women, he gives a shortened version of the angel's message. The word our Bible translates "hail," *chairete*, literally means "rejoice." In the imperative, Jesus commands them, "You rejoice!"

Like the woman with ointment (26:6-13), these women fall at Jesus' feet. The word "worshiped" means they prostrated themselves before Jesus. This worship is characteristic of Matthew's gospel; he uses the term twelve times. (It occurs only twice in the other synoptic gospels.) The proper response to an Oriental king is homage and prostration.

And the proper response of a king is to reassure his subjects: "Do not be afraid." Further, the man Jesus, who is now the resurrected Christ, needs to remind them that they are still brethren, *adelphois*. The plural is used to include both sexes. In the words of the Letter to the Hebrews, "For he who sanctifies and those who are sanctified have all one origin. That is why he is not ashamed to call them brethren" (Heb. 2:11).

Here, again, are the four great motifs already introduced in the chapter: Rejoice, don't fear, go tell, you will see. God leaves nothing to chance. This fourfold message is announced by an angel and then, to assure emphasis and clarity, is declared by the Lord himself.

We sometimes miss the point the first time around. God provides second chances. Week after week, God invites us to a feast that heals our sorrows and drives away our fears. Jesus reminds us by means of his Table that we are still his brothers and sisters. Each week we have another opportunity to join with his family and be united in holy communion. Let us join the women of Galilee, and our brothers and sisters at every altar all over the world, and let us worship the Christ.

> Lord, enthroned in heavenly splendour,
> First-begotten from the dead,
> Thou alone, our strong defender,
> Liftest up thy people's head.
> Alleluia! Alleluia! Alleluia!
> Jesus, true and living Bread!
> Jesus, true and living Bread!
>
> Here our humblest homage pay we;
> Here in loving reverence bow;
> Here for faith's discernment pray we
> Lest we fail to know thee now.

Alleluia! Alleluia! Alleluia!
Thou art here, we ask not how,
Thou art here, we ask not how.

Life imparting heavenly Manna,
Stricken Rock with streaming side,
Heaven and earth with loud hosanna
Worship Thee, the Lamb who dies.

Alleluia! Alleluia! Alleluia!
Risen, ascended, glorified!
Risen, ascended, glorified!

(George H. Bourne, 1840-1925)

Matthew 28:11-15

[11]While they were going, behold, some of the guard went into the city and told the chief priests all that had taken place. [12]And when they had assembled with the elders and taken counsel, they gave a sum of money to the soldiers [13]and said, "Tell people, 'His disciples came by night and stole him away while we were asleep.' [14]And if this comes to the governor's ears, we will satisfy him and keep you out of trouble." [15]So they took the money and did as they were directed; and this story has been spread among the Jews to this day.

Here Matthew completes the story begun in 27:62-66 and accounts for a common rumor in the first century, that

Jesus was not resurrected, but his body was stolen by disciples who then declared him risen. (This charge is referred to in Justin Martyr and in Tertullian.) As the women have run to tell the disciples the good news, some of the guards have apparently wakened from their "trance" and now must go and report this amazing turn of events to the high priests. They are not in an enviable position!

If Jesus is risen from the dead, then there is no excuse not to believe his claims. The priests, faced with the fact that they have killed an innocent man, must continue to hide the truth. They offer to pay off the guards, as they paid off Judas Iscariot, to circulate a lie. For a Roman soldier to be asleep on watch was punishable by death. In the climax of their story of deception, the chief priests and elders make it look as if they are protecting the guards when they are, in fact, protecting themselves.

The falsity and self-interest of the high priests and elders stands in stark contrast to the truth and selflessness of the Lord. The things of darkness and secrets of the heart are finally uncovered. What is true and noble endures, and the shallow and selfish disappears.

On the altar are symbols of the Lord's self-giving. In flesh and blood, we see the truth that endures: "For whoever would save his life will lose it; and whoever loses his life for my sake and the gospel's will save it" (Mark 8:35; cf. Matt. 10:39; Luke 17:33). Jesus gave up what was rightfully his that we might have what could never otherwise be ours. What we celebrate is not self-preservation but self-giving. Thank God!

Matthew 28:16-17

¹⁶Now the eleven disciples went to Galilee, to the mountain to which Jesus had directed them. ¹⁷And when they saw him they worshiped him; but some doubted.

Even if they had not been so directed, it would have been natural for the disciples to return to Galilee. Galilee was "home"; it represented the normal continuation of ministry in everyday circumstances. However, they return to "the mountain to which Jesus had directed them." Our minds drift back to the place of the Sermon on the Mount or to the mount of transfiguration. Mountains are places of revelation. (Here we see a continuance of Matthew's attempt to help us see Jesus as a new Moses.)

Jesus apparently appears on the mountain as the angel of Mark 16:7 predicted. As he is revealed to them, they "worshiped" him; again, this is characteristic of Matthew. And then there is the troubling—and realistic—reminder, "but some doubted." The Greek word *distazo* is the same one Matthew chose to describe Peter's lack of faith in 14:31: "O man of little faith, why did you doubt?"

The question is as valid today as it was then. Why, when confronted with Jesus Christ, do some worship and some doubt? Perhaps it is because some merely look and do not go on to listen. As Gerhard Barth points out, the focus of this passage is not the appearance, but the words of Jesus that follow. Jesus "came and said" (v. 18). "The meaning therefore can only be that this doubt is overcome by the word of Jesus."[26]

Likewise, we can merely look at this Table and doubt its power and his presence. Or we can hear his word: "This do," and participate in the meal. As the word follows the appearance, so our action follows his command. We take bread and break it. We pour out water and wine. His Table invites us, "O taste and see that the LORD is good! Happy is the man who takes refuge in him" (Ps. 34:8). Or, in the words of Jesus, "Blessed are those who have not seen and yet believe" (John 20:29).

Matthew 28:18-20

[18] And Jesus came and said to them, "All authority in heaven and on earth has been given to me. [19] Go therefore and make disciples of all nations, baptizing them in the name of the Father and of the Son and of the Holy Spirit, [20] teaching them to observe all that I have commanded you; and lo, I am with you always, to the close of the age."

Last words always convey unusual power and poignancy. This is also true of Jesus' last words as recorded in Matthew. Jesus tells his disciples that in the transformation after his suffering, all authority has been given to him. Therefore, because he has this power, all nations, not just the house of Israel, are to be made his disciples by baptizing them into the triune name. By baptism into this name, the baptized receive its power and become subject to its demands.

The teaching, which is always focal in Matthew, follows baptizing. Christ is to be made known through the proclamation of his teaching. And when we do this, as he commands, he is with us. (Compare John 14—16.) This is the meaning of the name God gives Jesus in the beginning of the gospel: "His name will be called Emmanuel (which means, God with us)" (Matt. 1:23).

Every significant part of these verses comes from Matthew's special vocabulary and reflects his special, theological concerns. The gospel closes with the three great concerns it has raised. First: Authority has been given to Jesus so that he can proclaim the new law. (See the Sermon on the Mount.) Second: Disciples must be made, not just of Israel, but of all people. (See the Missionary Discourse.) Third: the presence of Jesus with the church through all times.

Today we feel his presence most closely when we gather at his Table. Here is his body and his blood; his Spirit, which empowers us for the task of disciple-making; and his people, who encourage us in like-minded fellowship. Truly, this Table was given to fulfill what was spoken by the greatest Prophet, "Lo, I am with you always, to the close of the age."

> From the table now retiring
> Which for us the Lord hath spread,
> May our souls, refreshment finding,
> Grow in all things like our Head.
>
> His example while beholding,
> May our lives His image bear;
> Him our Lord and Master calling,
> His commands may we revere.
>
> Love to God and man displaying,
> Walking steadfast in His way,
> Joy attend us in believing,
> Peace from God thro' endless day.

(John Rowe, 1764-1833)

Notes

1. W. D. Davies, *The Setting of the Sermon on the Mount*. Cambridge University Press, 1966.
2. Robert Gundry, *Matthew: A Commentary on His Literary and Theological Art*. Eerdmans, 1982, pp. 609-622.
3. Several well-known scholars still hold the Griesbach hypothesis. Among them are Abbot C. Butler, William R. Farmer, Michael D. Goulder, and C. S. Mann.
4. Jack D. Kingsbury, *Matthew*. Fortress, 1977. For a popular explanation of the Hebrew theory see George Howard, "Was the Gospel of Matthew Originally Written in Hebrew?" *Bible Review*, Vol. 2, No. 4 (Winter 1986), pp. 14-25.
5. For a discussion of the M material see B. H. Streeter, *The Four Gospels: A Study of Origins*. London: Macmillan, 1951.
6. Benjamin Bacon, *Studies in Matthew*. London: Henry Holt & Co., 1930.
7. Bornkamm, Barth, and Held, *Tradition and Interpretation in Matthew*. Westminster, 1963.
8. Matthew's five discourses are generally held to be the Sermon on the Mount (5:1-7, 27), the Missionary Discourse (10:5-42), the Teaching in Parables (13:1-52), the Regulations for Christian Community (18:1-35), and the Apocalyptic Discourse (24—25). These discourses close with some version of the formula, "when Jesus had finished these sayings."
9. For a meditation on "delivered up" see Matt. 27:1-2.
10. For the use of perfumes in burial see 2 Chron. 16:14.
11. A summary of the literature on this issue is found in David Hill, *The Gospel of Matthew* (NCBC). Eerdmans, 1984, pp. 335-337.
12. Gundry, *Matthew*, pp. 524-525.
13. "Iscariot" has been interpreted as a transliteration of *sycharites*, thus linking Judas with the zealots. It may mean an inhabitant of Keriot or of Jericho (due to a corruption): It may also be

a transposition of the Aramaic *sheqarya*, "false one" or "deceiver." See Hill, *The Gospel of Matthew*, p. 338.

14. A. Carr, *The Gospel According to St. Matthew*. Cambridge University Press, 1905, p. 200.

15. F. E. Hutchinson, *The Works of George Herbert*. Oxford: Clarendon Press, 1972, pp. 188-189.

16. LeRoy Lawson, *The Lord of Parables*. Cincinnati: Standard Publishing Co., 1978, p. 67.

17. Gundry, *Matthew*, pp. 558-560.

18. Bruce M. Metzger, *A Textual Commentary on the Greek New Testament*. London: United Bible Societies, 1975, pp. 67-68.

19 Our term "Calvary" comes from the Latin *calvaria*, bare skull.

20. Many of the details of the Passion in Matthew also occur in Psalm 22. The reader will find it helpful to review that Psalm at this point and to keep it in mind hereafter.

21. From the note on Psalm 22:1 in the *New International Version Study Bible*. Zondervan, 1984, p. 805.

22. *Book of Common Prayer*. Oxford University Press, 1979, p. 339.

23. Some ancient sources add to Matthew 27:49b "And another took a spear and pierced his side, and out came water and blood." See also John 19:31-37.

24. M. R. James, trans., *The Apocryphal New Testament*. Oxford: Clarendon Press, 1953, p. 91.

25. Fred B. Craddock, *The Gospels*. Abingdon, 1982, p. 121.

26. Bornkamm, Barth, and Held, *Tradition and Interpretation in Matthew*, p. 132.

Works Consulted

Allen, Willoughby C., *The Gospel According to St. Matthew*. Edinburgh: T. &. T. Clark, 1922.

Bacon, B.W., *Studies in Matthew*. Holt, 1930.

Barclay, William, *The First Three Gospels*. Westminster, 1975.

Book of Common Prayer of the Protestant Episcopal Church in the U.S.A. Oxford University Press, 1979.

Bornkamm, Günther, Barth, Gerhard, and Held, Heinz, *Tradition and Interpretation in Matthew*. Westminster, 1963.

Butler, B.C., *The Originality of St. Matthew*. Cambridge University Press, 1951.

Carmichael, Ralph, et. al., *The New Church Hymnal*. Lexicon Music, 1976.

Carr, A., *The Gospel According to St. Matthew*. Cambridge University Press, 1905.

Christian Worship: A Hymnal. Bethany Press, 1953.

Craddock, Fred B., *The Gospels*. Abingdon, 1982

Dahl, Nils A., *Jesus in the Memory of the Early Church*. Augsburg, 1976.

Ellis, Peter F., *Matthew: His Mind and His Message*. Collegeville: Liturgical Press, 1985.

Erdman, Charles R., *The Gospel of Matthew: An Exposition*. Westminster, 1920.

Gundry, Robert, *Matthew*. Eerdmans, 1982

Harrington, Daniel J. S.J., *The Gospel According to Matthew*. Collegeville: Liturgical Press, 1983.

Hill, David. *The Gospel of Matthew*. Eerdmans, 1984.

Hymnal of the Protestant Episcopal Church in the U.S.A. New York: Church Pension Fund, 1940.

James, M.R., trans., *The Apocryphal New Testament*. Oxford: Clarendon Press, 1953.

Kee, H.C., Young, F.W., and Froelich, K., *Understanding the New Testament*. Prentice-Hall, 1965.

Kilpatrick, G.D., *The Origins of the Gospel According to St. Matthew*. Oxford: Clarendon Press, 1946.

Lawson, LeRoy, *The Lord of Parables*. Cincinnati, Standard Publishing Co., 1978.

McGarvey, J.W., *Matthew and Mark* (N. T. Commentary, Vol. 1). St. Louis: Christian Publishing Co., 1875.

McNeile, Alan H., *The Gospel According to St. Matthew*. Macmillan, 1955.

Metzger, Bruce, *A Textual Commentary on the Greek New Testament*. London: United Bible Societies, 1975.

Mineart, Paul S., *Matthew: The Teacher's Gospel*. London: Dartman, Longman & Todd, 1984.

Perrin, Norman, and Duling, *The New Testament: An Introduction*. Harcourt, Brace, Jovanovich, 1982.

Rienecker, Fritz, and Rogers, Cleon, *Linguistic Key to the New Testament*. Zondervan, 1976.

Smith, B.T.D., *The Gospel According to St. Matthew*. Cambridge University Press, 1950.

Stanley, David M., S.J., *The Gospel of St. Matthew*. Collegeville: Liturgical Press, 1963.

www.ingramcontent.com/pod-product-compliance
Lightning Source LLC
Chambersburg PA
CBHW060422090426
42734CB00011B/2403